The Last Lorry

Kelvin Hughes

For
Beni, David and Sandra
with love...
...for as long as forever is...

ONE

The last lorry left Madrid just before dawn. Only a few hours later, the first of Franco's troops began to enter the shattered city, looking for the last pockets of resistance but finding almost none. The city that had held out so desperately for so many months had finally had enough. The end when it came was surprisingly quick and surprisingly easy, everyone just wanted the war to be over. But the war was still going on. There was still some sort of organised resistance farther south, although of course it was futile.

The lorry picked its way carefully around the barricades of the outer suburbs and headed south, slowly, its load heavy, its destination a long way off. A mean rain fell. Captain Daniel Gonzalez felt his body being jolted to and fro as the lorry stumbled over the debris that littered the highway and lurched from pothole to pothole. Beside him, the driver, Paco, fought with the wheel like a maniac, peering ahead through the grey rain, trying to avoid the worst of the pitfalls in front of them. But it made little difference which way he turned. And beside the road in a never-ending stream trudged the people, fleeing. Heads bowed, wrapped in scarves and blankets, some carrying their meagre possessions in hastily prepared bundles, they trudged ever onward. Everyone was heading south, away from the sound of the war that was closing in all around them. This last southern corridor remained, but it wouldn't be open for long, and everyone knew it.

*

Dani had been asleep on a thin mattress in a shuttered room at the barracks when Nando had burst in to wake him. It was the first time he had closed his eyes in days and the first time he had been able to sleep lying down in weeks. He had almost forgotten about the war, almost, but just as the last traces of it were exiting his mind so he was forced awake again.

"Dani, Dani, wake up!" barked Nando rocking him violently, gripping his shoulders and rolling him over onto his back.

"Mierda!" exclaimed the young Captain, "what the hell's happened?"

"The General's sent a car for you, hurry, it's urgent."

"The General? Which General? I don't know any generals."

"Of course you do, come on. You don't want to keep him waiting. The driver says you're needed for a special mission."

"He sent a car? I didn't know there was any petrol left."

"It must be an important mission then, mustn't it?"

"The only missions left in this war are suicide ones and the only bastard stupid enough left to take them is me."

Dani got wearily up from his mattress on the floor and rubbed his tired face with both hands.

"I could do with a wash and a shave," he decided, "and so could you my friend," he added looking at Fernando.

"I could do with a couple of hours soaking in a bath, a good breakfast of ham and eggs and a pretty malagueña to wash and iron my uniform, but we don't have time. The driver said to bring our kit with us we won't be coming back here."

"You mean we won't be coming back alive."

"Maybe we're being sent away from Madrid, maybe we're to be saved."

"Maybe there's a new kind of bomb they've invented which you have to strap to a captain's back and leave him to blow up when the enemy tanks roll over him – that seems more likely."

"Whatever it is it's urgent, so get a move on."

"I'll just have a quick wash," he told his adjutant, "you get my kit together." He went over to a bowl of cold water and splashed some up into his eyes. Fernando picked up the Captain's small diary from the floor beside the straw-filled mattress and pushed it into a large kitbag and they were ready to leave.

Outside, Dani was surprised to discover that it was still dark. In fact, it was so dark that it had to be the middle of the night. He looked at his watch and saw that it was two in the morning. No wonder he felt like shit, he hadn't even been asleep for two hours. Today was rumoured to be the last day of the siege, the city had had all it could take, and resistance was thought to be about to end. No doubt the General wanted to get it over with as quickly as possible, perhaps before breakfast. Dani hoped that he had not been chosen as the man to walk out from the lines carrying the white flag. But that was the thought that was starting to nag away at his brain, now that it was beginning to return to life. Please don't let it be me, he begged of no one in particular. He didn't want his war to end with him being the man who had to give up this city, this city that had vowed never to surrender. Had it all been for this? All these endless months of deprivation, all the bloodshed, all the violence, all for nothing? *No pasarán* they had said, but now the city was doomed.

The driver cursed and spat as he gingerly manoeuvred the staff car around the worst of the bomb craters and tried to avoid getting a puncture from the stray slabs of stone that had once been part of the pavement. It was a dangerous journey, always at the top speed the driver could manage between road blocks, but danger was a normal everyday thing now, and the three men were unconcerned even when a stray bomb fell in the next street away to their right and lit up the night with fire.

They reached the General's latest headquarters in the basement of a once fine apartment building which had had its upper floors blown away during an air raid. The driver took them inside through some heavy wooden doors and across an interior patio where soldiers were sleeping hunched up against the stone walls. Someone was snoring loudly, someone else muttering a girl's name, another man was whimpering like a small dog. They went down a flight of steps into the darkness of the basement and the driver led them down a corridor to the General's office. He knocked once and then showed Dani inside, whilst he and Fernando remained in the corridor.

The General was sitting at his desk shrouded in a pall of dark grey smoke, a permanent cigarette hanging from the corner of his mouth. His face was deathly white and his cheeks sunken.

"Comrade General," said Dani, raising his clenched fist in salute.

"Comrade Captain," muttered the General although he made no effort to return the salute or to get up from his chair. The General was signing a document that looked like a set of orders, and when he finished he stamped it with a loud thump of his official seal.

"Captain Gonzalez," began the General, peering through the fug of smoke, his small dead eyes almost obscured behind the dirty lenses of his round glasses. "I have chosen you for a mission of the utmost importance. It is dangerous of course, but then these are dangerous times. I know your loyalty is beyond question and since your arrival from

Malaga your commitment to the cause has not gone unnoticed, that is why you have been selected."

"Thank you Comrade General," said Dani although he wouldn't be thankful at all if this was all a build up to him being given the white flag mission. He wondered if he could refuse to be a part of the surrender, but then the General would probably just have him taken up to the patio and one of the soldiers there would be woken to take him out into the street and shoot him. There were plenty of dead bodies already littered around one more would make no difference to anyone.

"Yes, yes," continued the General, somewhat annoyed at having been interrupted. "As I was saying, this mission is of vital importance and very urgent. As I'm sure you are aware the Rebels are about to take the city, further resistance is impossible, and therefore we must save what we can from the enemy. Your orders are to take a lorry down to Alicante. The lorry will be disguised as an ambulance, but it will be carrying a valuable cargo, a very valuable cargo. A cargo you are to protect at all costs. Once you reach Alicante you will find a ship waiting at the port for you."

"Yes, Comrade General."

"You are to avoid the main highway south, keep to the back roads and do not let this cargo fall into the hands of the enemy. As soon as the Rebels enter Madrid they will come looking for it, and when they realise it is gone they will stop at nothing to capture it, do you understand?"

"Perfectly," responded Dani although he didn't understand at all.

"It's all here in your orders, make sure you don't fail. We've found a British nurse to accompany you on your mission, frankly we want her out of the city before it falls. We don't want a foreign woman caught up in this. You'll also need to take someone with you disguised as a patient for when you get stopped at road blocks. These orders should get you through to begin with, but who knows what the next few days hold in store."

"I'll take my adjutant Comrade General."

"Is he trustworthy?"

"I've known him since I was a boy. We grew up in the same street in Malaga."

"Good. Well then, all that remains is to wish you luck. The legitimate government of Spain is counting on you. Viva la Republica!"

"Viva la Republica," echoed Dani raising his clenched fist.

"My driver will take you to where the lorry is waiting, it's already loaded. The cargo is in sealed containers, on no account are they to be opened, on no account, do you understand?"

"Yes Comrade General."

"You must not let this cargo fall into the hands of the enemy. You will be given dynamite and should the need arise you are to blow up the lorry and everything in it. You might as well blow yourself up with it for that matter."

The lorry was waiting in a small square at the rear of the General's Headquarters. It was an ugly-looking thing with two metal bars to protect the engine at the front but it certainly looked powerful and strong. It was an American-made lorry, one of eighteen that had belatedly been donated to the Republican cause to serve as ambulances. It had a large red cross painted on each side and one on its roof to signal to enemy aircraft its purpose. Dani wondered just how long the disguise might protect them.

The English nurse was there and she introduced herself as Elizabeth. She looked tired and worried, but then didn't everyone in Madrid? Her uniform was clean and pressed and seemed out of place amongst the rubble and debris of the square. Dani shook the delicate white hand she offered him and greeted her in English.

"They didn't tell me you were English," she said, a look of pleasant surprise transforming her face. "They said your name was Captain Gonzalez."

"It is, well, no it isn't really. My father's surname is Miller, he is, was, English" said Dani, "it's just easier in this war to be Gonzalez, that way there are no explanations needed."

"Well, I'm pleased to meet you Comrade Captain."

"Dani," he told her. "And this is your patient, Fernando."

"He doesn't look wounded to me."

"He isn't. You'll need to do something about that."

"Sure, I've got some bandages with me."

"Whatever you do I want his arm in a big sling with his revolver hidden inside."

"I think we can do that."

"Good. Now, let's check out the cargo shall we," he said to Fernando, switching naturally back into Spanish, something he had always done throughout his childhood.

"It's all loaded ready," put in the driver who had been standing nearby, not wishing to interrupt as the Captain and the nurse had been speaking in a language he couldn't understand and therefore he wasn't sure if what they were saying was important or not.

"Where did you pick it up?"

"I didn't Comrade Captain, it was already loaded when it was delivered here this evening. The man who gave me the keys wouldn't tell me what we're carrying he only said it was bloody heavy."

Fernando drew back the tarpaulin curtains that covered the back of the lorry and dropped the tailgate. Then he stepped aside for Dani to climb up first. It was dark and there was no moonlight since the sky was covered by dirty black rain clouds.

"Have you got a torch," Dani called out to the driver.

"I'll see if there's one in the cab," responded Paco and he went to look. He returned a minute later with a heavy industrial torch. "These Americans think of everything," he laughed. He put on the light and held it up to the Captain who was already inside the lorry. Taking the heavy torch, Dani did a sweep of the interior. There were two stretchers placed on top of tarpaulin sheets which were obviously there to conceal the cargo that had been loaded on each side of the lorry with a passageway left in the middle. Cautiously Dani raised the corner of one of the sheets. Underneath there were metal crates, stacked together. Pulling the cover right up, he saw that there were six crates along the floor with another six placed on top. They were lashed tightly together with rope. He examined the nearest crate and saw that it had a heavy padlock on it.

"I don't suppose they gave you the keys to these padlocks did they?" he called out.

"No, they didn't," replied the driver, "they told me not to let anyone open them. If anyone tries I'm to shoot them. Even you, Comrade Captain."

"Then I guess we're not going to find out what's inside until we reach Alicante," sighed Dani.

"Alicante?" asked the nurse.

"Didn't they tell you?"

"No, they just said I was leaving Madrid, that's all."

"Just in time too," put in Fernando, "it's all going to be over in a few hours."

"It's so sad," said the nurse.

Dani continued his inspection of the back of the lorry and found some cans of fuel, four blankets and a small wooden box containing a couple of sticks of dynamite, just as the General had promised. What could their cargo possibly be that made it of such great value? If he knew what it was then maybe he would be able to decide if it was worth dying for or not, but then again his orders told him that it was, and that would have to suffice.

The Captain jumped down from the back of the lorry and decided it was time to get going, the sooner they were out of Madrid the better. They had a long journey ahead of them, and if they were to travel by night and avoid the main route south then it would take them a lot longer. What worried Dani most, apart from the mysterious nature of their cargo, was just how long the doomed Republic could continue to hold out. As soon as the Rebels took the capital they would surely waste no time in pressing south, forcing what resistance remained into a small pocket around Valencia and Alicante from where there could be no escape. As a Captain of the Republican army Dani knew well enough that if he were captured he would be shot. They might torture him first. They might starve him almost to death in some freezing cell, but eventually he would be taken somewhere and shot. The thought sent a chill down his spine.

*

As a feeble sun began to chase away the rain clouds at dawn, so Paco turned the lorry off the main highway south and they headed into the country looking for somewhere to hide up for the day. It had been a long, tense night for all of them and they could do with some rest. Besides, as soon as it was properly light the enemy might have planes up looking for them if what they were carrying was really as important as they had been led to believe. It was also very possible that someone in Madrid would betray them. Someone had to know what was in these metal crates on this American lorry, and that information might just save their life. Who wouldn't hesitate to give away any secret in return for their freedom, or for the safety of their family?

They found a track that led away from the road and in the distance there was a small group of tall trees, and there they parked up for the day, the lorry hidden beneath a canopy of leaves. The English nurse slept in the back of the lorry on one of the stretchers whilst the three men lay on blankets on the ground. Dani dozed for a while and was awoken by a midday sun which filtered through a gap in the leaves above and played across his face. There were birds squabbling over mates in the higher branches and he realized that it was now spring. In Madrid there had been no more trees and no birds, and therefore no spring, and the sun had often been obscured by the drifting smoke from burning buildings, fires that no one cared to put out. And yet here, beneath these tall trees beside a dried-up stream, it was possible to believe that there had never been a war and that things were just as they had always been, just as they always should have been.

He lay awake for a long time. He thought about writing something in his diary, but he was enjoying just listening to the sounds of peace that he hadn't heard for over two years. Could his country ever get back to what it had once been he wondered, or would the scars of this vicious civil war remain forever? He knew that his life could never be as it had been before. His parents had both been killed during the Italian bombardment of Malaga. Their little flat just off the Alameda Principal had been blasted away, and with it had gone all his happy childhood memories, almost as if a bomb had exploded in his heart. He had begged them to leave, but they had refused. And they had died together in their tiny flat surrounded by a lifetime of possessions that in the end amounted to almost nothing.

Dani's father had been a young soldier in the Great War, had been gassed near Ypres and almost died. When he finally got out of hospital he was advised to go and live somewhere sunny, which the doctors thought might help his lungs to recover from the terrible effects of the gas he had inhaled. He ended up in Malaga working at the Academia Berlitz in the Alameda Principal, teaching English to the children of the upper classes. One of his first pupils had been the eldest daughter of a wealthy local businessman, just eighteen, and he had fallen in love with her at first sight. Whether she had felt the same Dani didn't know, his mother had never spoken about her feelings in front of him, but whether she loved him from the first moment they met or whether she had grown to love him over the next few months it didn't matter. After a year they were married and her father bought them their flat to live in, although he could not have approved of his daughter's choice of husband. And there they remained, quite happy as far as Dani could remember, until the arrival of the Italian Blackshirts.

Dani had seen the ruins of his childhood home just before his unit had been ordered to abandon the city and flee along the coast road to Almeria. He would rather have stayed there in the rubble of his parent's apartment block and choked to death in the dust, but his life-long friend, Fernando Fernández, had put a strong arm around his shoulders and led him away. They had looked back, through tears, from their open troop truck, at the smouldering remains of their beloved home city as they rattled along with the blue sea beside them. At the precise moment that the city had finally disappeared from view, a part of Daniel had died.

TWO

As soon as it was considered safe to do so, Captain Roberto Ruiz Roman had a car drive him towards the city centre. He was amazed to see how the buildings had suffered in the months of air raids and bombardment, and he realized that the Madrid he had known before the war was now gone. Nearly all the remaining buildings on this side of the city were damaged, and there were plenty of gaps where huge apartment blocks had once stood. It was amazing, he reflected, how this city had remained like a thorn in Franco's side for so long. It had become the symbol of the Republic's resistance and attracted great international attention, but now, at last, it had been captured. There was already talk of a huge victory parade as soon as the central streets could be cleared, and General Franco would make his long-awaited entry into the Spanish capital, triumphant. There would be a huge celebration, already the civilian population was beginning to emerge from the cellars and the tunnels of the metro system where they had been in hiding. No doubt they would make a big show of welcoming the victors. They would all claim to be members of Madrid's infamous Fifth Column that had been helping the Nationalist cause from within the capital throughout the war.

Roberto knew that the process of rounding up so-called Reds would soon begin, but for once he would not be a part of it as he had been in other captured cities, at least not until his current mission was over. It was a strange mission, just to check out a rumour really. He would make some enquiries in his normal subtle way and the thing would be resolved within a matter of hours. Then he could get back to the task of sniffing out Reds. As Franco himself was reported to have said, "better dead than red," and Captain Ruiz felt exactly the same way. If there was the slightest doubt in his mind about a person's allegiance then he would have them shot. He didn't want someone he had interrogated and set free coming back to kill him, so it was better to work on the assumption that everyone who was accused of a crime was guilty. They were all guilty of having chosen the wrong side at least. He was especially ruthless to any officers who had once been part of the Spanish regular army before the war and who had sided with the Republic rather than join the uprising.

They were the worst traitors of all. They had fought against their brother officers. It had been an uprising of the army and they should have joined. He liked nothing more than to hear them whimpering like frightened children just before they were shot. Some called for their mothers, some pissed themselves all of them regretted not joining the rebels.

He wondered how long it would take Madrid to get back on its feet. When would the trams be running properly again? When would the bars and cafés reopen? When would there be enough food in the shops? He knew there were bread lorries going around giving out Nationalist bread to the civilian population, it was an easy way to win them over to the new regime. Those who were close to starvation would welcome it most of all, as would mothers with small children, and so a fragile peace could begin. And all the time the hunt for hidden Reds would continue, remorselessly.

As the young Captain looked through the car window he found himself wondering for the first time since the outbreak of war about the future. For the last two years he had existed only on a daily basis, after all, each day was potentially his last, but now that the war was nearing a conclusion, so he was able to start to think ahead. He had always been a career soldier, like his father before him, and he saw no reason not to continue in the army when the fighting was over. There was talk of a European war already looming on the horizon, so it was possible that Spain would be involved in that. They had certainly gathered a lot of warfare experience during the campaigns they had fought, and presumably they would align themselves with the Germans and Italians who had come to fight in Spain. A European war would be just the ticket.

Captain Ruiz had his driver pull over outside an impressive building in the heart of the city's business area. Here there was some evidence of the air raids that had taken place in late 1936, windows were boarded up and some of the taller buildings were damaged. But now there was just an eerie quiet in these first hours of Nationalist occupation. This was once the busiest area of the Spanish capital, now it was almost a ghost town.

"Wait here," he commanded the driver, and he strode purposefully up a flight of stone steps towards the main entrance which was being casually guarded by a couple of soldiers. Among the first units to enter the city was a special detachment that had been briefed to make all haste to this area and secure all the important buildings. Their task was to save important documents and valuables from being destroyed or looted.

On entering the building, Captain Ruiz saw that the men had arrived just in time. There were several dead bodies lying around the large entrance foyer and pieces of paper strewn all over the marble floor. But, Roberto wasn't interested in paperwork.

*

Elizabeth climbed down from the back of the lorry just after midday. She had dozed a little, but for a long time had been awake listening to the men, trying to work out what they were saying but without much success. Her Spanish had improved a great deal in the time she had been in the country, but she was still far from fluent. She had a good medical vocabulary, she could talk about war wounds and dysentery with the best of them, but she didn't have enough experience at talking about more normal things. Fernando had been sweet during the drive through the darkness the previous night, he had spoken slowly and patiently with her, letting her get used to his southern accent. But there had come a time when he had run out of things to say and she had had a headache from concentrating so much, and so they had both drifted off to sleep which was why she hadn't been able to sleep much during the morning.

On seeing the nurse, the men stopped their conversation.

"Sorry if we woke you," said Dani.

"Oh, no, I couldn't sleep. I thought I'd get some fresh air as well," she mumbled. "Is it safe to walk around here?"

"It's not safe anywhere. If you want to stretch your legs you'll have to keep under the trees, we don't want to be spotted by an aircraft. We'll move on again as soon as it's dark, in the meantime we'll just have to be bored I'm afraid."

"That's okay, I don't mind a bit of boredom, it's been pretty hectic the last few months in Madrid I haven't had a moment to think."

"Go stretch your legs a bit and then we'll see what we've got to eat between us."

"I've got some chocolate," she laughed, "an American who worked for Radio Madrid gave it to me last week just before he left. He told me to keep it for emergencies, and I guess this is an emergency situation."

"We'll have a feast then," said Dani. Beth walked away into the trees, slowly, and the three men watched her go.

"I just hope that if I ever get really injured I've got someone like that to look after me," sighed Fernando.

"Yeah, she's a real *guapa* that one," agreed the driver. "What on earth possessed her to come to a war like this I wonder?"

"Beats me," said Fernando, "I tried talking to her last night, but her Spanish isn't very good, and she didn't seem to want to talk much anyway. Dani can find out can't you Dani? You speak English."

"She'll tell us what she wants us to know. I'm not going to press her for details about her life. Besides, as soon as we get to Alicante she'll be gone. I'm sure they'll find a space for her on a boat."

"And what about us?" asked Fernando.

"We, comrade, will be left to hold back the enemy long enough for the important people to escape, and then we'll be captured and shot," the driver informed him sounding unconcerned.

"Is that what you think Dani?"

"I don't know Nando, there was talk in Madrid that the Russians would send ships to Alicante to take us all away, but I don't know for sure," replied the Captain.

"What? So we could end up in Russia?"

"It's either end up in Russia or end up dead," laughed Dani.

"I think I'd rather die," decided Paco the driver.

In the end their lunch consisted of a small tin of sardines, a hunk of stale bread, a piece of chorizo that Paco must have had in his pocket for weeks and a tiny sliver of American chocolate each. At first the men had been reluctant to take Elizabeth's chocolate, but she had insisted, and she had watched with delight the way their faces changed as each tasted it. None of them could remember ever having tasted anything so fine, maybe before the war started, and that seemed like so long ago. Dani could only remember having chocolate at the feria when his wealthy grandfather had bought him some. It had seemed to him then as a little taste of heaven, and so it was now. They sat in silence for a long time after eating the chocolate, each lost in their own thoughts. Finally they dozed off in the cool shade of the trees as the heat of the afternoon began to boil around their little oasis.

They were awoken a couple of hours later by the drone of an approaching aircraft. Dani rose up onto his knees and tried to make out through the gaps in the canopy of leaves above whether it was an enemy plane or one of their own. It was impossible to get a good view, but he was glad about that since it meant that the pilot would not be able to see them either. It was unlikely to be a Republican aircraft now. Most had been shot down or destroyed as their bases had been captured. Dani wondered if the plane was searching specifically for them, or if it was out on a routine patrol or perhaps the pilot was just lost.

The plane buzzed around for a few minutes during which they all held their breath, and then, at last, the rattle of its engine receded and it went away towards the north.

*

Captain Roberto Ruiz Roman wiped some blood from his forehead. He played with it casually between his fingers, it was warm and sticky. He looked at the shattered face of the man who lay on the floor whimpering at his feet. It always amazed him just how much a human body could take and still continue to live. This man had been beaten continuously for nearly two hours. They had burnt him with cigarettes, punched and kicked him, pissed on him, held his head under water and almost drowned him in a big sink and beaten him with a wooden plank, and still the bastard hadn't talked. Finally, the Captain had lost patience and grabbing the man's hair he had begun to repeatedly smash his face down against a marble work surface. They were using the little kitchen as their interrogation room since it offered a wider variety of possibilities for pain than a normal room. They had used a large knife to cut the man's face so it appeared that he was crying blood, and also to hack off the little finger of his right hand, but his screaming had got on their nerves and that was when Roberto had snapped. He had smashed the man's face repeatedly against the marble, destroying the nose and pulping the skin of the man's forehead and cheeks. The man's teeth lay on the floor and blood was everywhere.

Roberto had decided that the man wasn't going to talk and would have kept up the beating until he was dead, but his assistant, the soldier who had been assigned as his driver, pulled him away and screamed at him that the man wanted to talk. It was extremely difficult to work out what was being said. Roberto had lost all patience, but at last the man managed to tell them that a lorry had taken what they were looking for, a few hours earlier. Roberto cursed his bad luck. Still, there was only one way for it to have gone, the only road that was still open led south to where the remnants of the Republican army would probably make their futile last stand. It shouldn't be too difficult to find a large heavy lorry moving south, although the highway would no doubt be a mass of fleeing civilians. He would send a plane up to look for it straight away. General Franco himself was interested in this matter and Captain Roberto Ruiz had orders that allowed him to use any means possible to complete his mission.

The man on the floor had stopped whimpering now and was desperately trying to speak again. Roberto crouched down and put his ear next to the toothless mouth.

"Kill me you bastard," snarled the man through his agony. For a moment Roberto considered making his victim suffer a little bit more. Maybe there were other things the man could tell him. Normally he might have enjoyed cutting off a bit of an ear or gouging out an eye, but his orders were pressing. So, reluctantly, he drew his pistol placed it against the man's temple and blew him away. A mixture of brains and blood splattered all over his uniform and he spat at the body in disgust. It was time to leave. He would shower and change and head out to the aerodrome and get a plane up as soon as possible. He had wasted too much time getting the information he needed, he mustn't let the lorry and its important cargo get too much of a start on him.

THREE

At dusk, Dani helped Paco the driver fill the lorry's petrol tank from one of the large cans they carried in the back. He wondered if they had been given enough petrol to get them all the way to their destination, but he didn't ask the other man's opinion since he was afraid of the answer. He already had enough on his mind. Would it be possible to obtain more petrol along their route? Somehow he doubted it. With over two years of war behind them, everything was in short supply, food, arms, ammunition, uniforms, but especially petrol. They hadn't seen any other motor vehicles on the road the previous night, just an endless stream of weary refugees, walking, heads bowed, carrying their possessions in sheets hung over their backs. They dragged their skeletal, uncomplaining children along behind them. With the sound of the approaching lorry, these ghost-like people would shuffle over to the side of the road and stare with frightened eyes. They had no way of knowing whether this was the last of their retreating army or the first of the advancing enemy. Everyone had heard stories of what the Rebels had done to the civilian populations of the towns and cities they had captured.

As the lorry had passed scattered groups of refugees during the night so some had reached out towards the cab, imploring the driver to take pity on them and offer them a ride to some imagined salvation. Others, seeing the red-cross insignia, called out for medical aid for their dying children. Fortunately, Elizabeth riding in the back was not able to understand the shouted pleas of the people above the spluttering of the engine and the creaking of the canvas. Had she been able to, it would have broken her heart.

They were just about to climb into the back of the lorry and get Fernando bandaged up for the night, when they heard the returning hum of the aircraft. They froze, still, barely daring to breathe, listening, as the lone machine stumbled towards them. It was almost dark now and the pilot must surely be thinking about heading back to base. It was impossible to know for certain that the plane was up looking for them, but it sure felt like it. Elizabeth looked into Dani's eyes to see if there were any signs there of the fear she was feeling inside, but she saw no fear, only an emptiness that she hadn't expected. She realised that she had stopped breathing and let out a gasp. Immediately she clasped her hand over her mouth as if she thought that the noise would have given away their position. Dani chuckled quietly and she realised what she had done and she smiled at him. His eyes no longer seemed empty. She found herself wondering what this tired-looking young man had been through during this war, and what was it that inspired his loyalty to a cause that was now so utterly lost.

The plane's single engine spluttered and coughed, and for a couple of seconds it seemed that it might be about to stop all together, but then it roared back into life and the pilot turned and throttled away, back towards Madrid. Dani watched the plane until it was completely swallowed up by the blackening sky and he was sure that it wouldn't come around for another look.

"Let's get on the move shall we, I don't think he saw us, but you never know," he said. Elizabeth reached for the large bandage she had used the previous night to make Fernando's sling and he handed her a revolver to be hidden inside. Dani went to the cab and told Paco that they were ready to leave. The driver grunted and started the heavy engine to get them under way again. They hadn't covered a great distance the previous night because of their late start and because of the chaos at the road blocks on the way out of Madrid. It seemed that anything with wheels that could be pushed or pulled was leaving the capital. Old prams were crammed with family keepsakes, and small carts were pulled by old men. There were no horses left in Madrid, the last long winter of war had seen to that. Old women followed behind the carts, often carrying a straw-filled mattress on their heads, these being their most valuable possessions.

They went back along the track towards the road. Paco, the driver, reckoned that they were just beyond Arganda del Rey, as they had crossed the Jarama River in the early hours of the morning. Almost as soon as they began, the darkness closed in around them. In the distance Dani could just make out some of the taller hills like hump-backed sentinels lining their route as they descended slowly down into the valley towards the town of Perales de Tajuña. The lorry was heavy and the engine spluttered alarmingly at times, and Dani wondered how it would cope when they had to climb once more on the approach to Albacete.

In the back Elizabeth sat on one side and Fernando on the other. They swayed to and fro as the lorry jolted them along. They were silent, both lost in their own thoughts. Elizabeth now realised she might escape from Spain and go back to England. The last few months she had assumed she would stay in Madrid until the end. She felt like a traitor running away. She tried to imagine what the city must be going through, swarming with victorious Rebel soldiers, among them the dreaded Moors of the Foreign Legion. Would they be looting what little was left to take, or worse still would they be raping the women? She hoped her friends the Spanish nurses would be safe. She had been the last foreigner remaining when all the others had been allowed to leave. But she had insisted on staying. Maybe it was because she had nothing to return to, maybe it was because she still felt like there was something left for her to do in this war. Perhaps this mission was it. She couldn't begin to imagine what their secret cargo might be, but if there was just the slightest hope that it might help the Republic to survive then it had to arrive safely in Alicante.

Elizabeth was from a wealthy family and had been brought up in Bournemouth. As a girl she had always been happiest when she was looking out to sea, wondering if perhaps her future lay elsewhere, over the water. She wasn't content simply to promenade along the seafront, or walk out on the pier, or wander down the paths of East Cliff. She always felt restless. Her mother had been a nurse in the Great War, and Elizabeth had decided that nursing would be her way out of the life that everyone seemed to expect for her. When she reached eighteen and her father started to get interested in potential suitors, she announced her intention of going to London to train as a nurse. Her father forbade it of course, but Elizabeth's mother took her side as she had known she would. After all, had her mother not gone to be a nurse in the Great War then she would never have met the wounded young officer whom she later married. Eventually Elizabeth was allowed to leave the family home and go to London.

At the end of her training, still feeling as if her future lay elsewhere, she volunteered with several of her student-nurse companions to leave for besieged Madrid. She had never felt so excited in her life. When she arrived, she was stunned at how she found the city. After two years of being in the front line the Spanish capital was battered and broken. It had first been bombed in October of 1936 by German and Italian planes, but it was the major assault of November that year which had left so many scars. The German Condor legion had done most of the damage, and only essential repairs had been carried out since. There were still huge bomb craters in the middle of streets, gaps in the buildings where an apartment block had been completely destroyed, and façades of beautiful old houses with nothing left behind them. The main boulevards were kept clear, but the smaller side streets were littered with debris of all sorts. You could see the back of a broken chair, a table with one leg, the top of a door, bathroom tiles of all colours, but worst of all were the more personal items, an old sepia photograph in a damaged frame, a child's small coat burned and abandoned.

Nothing in Elizabeth's previous life could have prepared her for the job she had come to do, and at first the wounds of her patients terrified her. However, she quickly hardened as she had to in order to be able to carry on. Medical supplies were beginning to run out, surgeons were exhausted, and it fell to the nurses to try to keep the hospitals running. Often it broke Elizabeth's heart to see men dying before her eyes in such great pain when there was nothing left for her to give them. The doctors performed miracles on the operating tables only for their patients to die later through lack of medicines to fight infections.

Elizabeth didn't find in Madrid the spirit of that first year of the war when the Spanish capital had been like some sort of a beacon shining its light of defiance out to the whole world. The people had been determined and brave. Their slogan of 'No Pasarán' had been shouted out defiantly for the whole world to hear and young men in their thousands from all corners and all walks of life came to join the International Brigades. It was the introduction of the first of these Brigades that saved Madrid from falling to the Rebels at the end of November of that first year of war, but by the time Elizabeth arrived the Internationals were all gone, as all hope had gone from the people who had remained in Madrid. The civilian population had been encouraged to leave by the Defence Committee so that all food supplies could go to the army, but many had stayed, afraid to leave their houses or businesses, or those with simply nowhere else to go. They sheltered in the city's subway stations or in the cellars of their bombed out homes, living like animals on scraps as best they could.

It seemed strange to the English nurse to walk along the great boulevards of Madrid where the once important buildings now seemed to be bowed down in defeat. Had she known the Spanish capital in better times she would have found it vibrant and alive, almost as if it were not just the centre of Spain but the very centre of the universe. But when she arrived it was like a wounded animal, slowly dying, with the vultures already circling overhead.

*

At the recently-captured air base of Cuatro Vientos to the south of Madrid, Captain Roberto Ruiz Roman paced the tarmac near the ancient control tower, waiting for the last of his planes to return. The other two had found nothing, but the third was still to come back. It was getting dark and he was beginning to wonder if perhaps the plane had got into difficulties. He couldn't imagine that it had met any enemy planes as the last remaining Russian-supplied Chato fighters had been taken care of that very morning. Their pilots had preferred to be shot from the skies rather than to surrender their biplanes. A few aircraft that were not air-worthy had been set on fire by fleeing mechanics and some of these were still smouldering even now. Perhaps the idiot pilot had lost his way.

Just as he had given up hope and was walking back to his car he heard the distinct grumble of an aero engine. He turned and squinted up at the sky and was just able to make out the shape of a tiny Fiat CR.32 biplane as it descended from within a low black cloud. He watched impatiently as the pilot lined up an approach to the runway, his aircraft buffeted by the wind as a storm was brewing. With a violent final manoeuvre, just avoiding a wrecked Chato that had crashed at the end of the runway, the young flyer brought the plane safely down and taxied over to where the Captain was waiting for him.

The pilot climbed from the plane jumping onto the tarmac. He hardly had time to remove his helmet and goggles before Roberto reached him.

"Well?" he questioned.

"Nothing," replied the young pilot with an apologetic shrug of the shoulders.

"What do you mean nothing?"

"That's what I said. I looked all along the main road like you told us to, but there wasn't a large lorry of any description. In fact, there were hardly any motor vehicles at all."

"Christ man, are you lot blind? How can you not find a bloody great lorry?"

"Maybe they've taken another route."

"What other route could they possibly take? They must be out there somewhere you just didn't see them that's all. You'll have to go up again at first light. I'll speak to General Franco if I have to. I want ten planes up tomorrow, all day."

Just then the heavens opened and the rain began to fall like heavy curtains.

"Will that be all, Captain?" asked the pilot eager to get inside.

"I guess so. You'd better find it tomorrow or I'll have you all shot." Roberto turned and walked over to where his driver was waiting for him. Away in the distance a storm rumbled between the hills.

*

A few fat drops of rain hit the lorry's windscreen like exploding insects and then came the rumble of thunder booming around the hills.

"Just what we fucking need," cursed the driver. "It's hard enough to see what's up ahead as it is."

"Let's hope that it blows over fairly quickly," said Dani trying to peer up at the sky. A lightning bolt lit up the landscape just for a second and then they were plunged back into darkness. The rain began to fall in earnest, heavy and thick. In the back, under canvas the raindrops sounded almost like exploding bullets and the wind like a cracking whip. Elizabeth was terrified and had to hold her hand over her mouth to stop herself from crying out.

Through the watery beam of the headlights Paco and Dani could no longer see a road, instead, in just a matter of minutes, the road had become like a grey-brown river surging around the wheels and sucking them down into it. The driver could feel the heavy lorry beginning to slip, and then suddenly it was out of control, lurching downward. He fought with the wheel, but he no longer felt in control.

FOUR

Dani reached across and grabbed the steering wheel to help steady the lorry and Paco stamped down hard on the brake pedal, and between them they managed to keep the heavy vehicle on course. On either side of them were ditches full of the muddy water that was gushing off the road and just ahead the road was totally underwater. The lorry slowed as it reached the bottom of the gentle slope and then stuck fast in the mud at the bottom as the road turned and then began to climb once again.

Paco hit the accelerator but the only return was a slight lurch forward and then the back wheels began to spin themselves further into the mud. He stopped for a second, let the lorry settle and then accelerated hard once again. The back of the lorry slipped sideways slightly, but there was no forward movement.

"Try to reverse a bit," suggested Dani. Paco wrenched the gear stick into reverse and pressed his foot hard down once more. Just for a second the lorry seemed to want to pull itself out of the mud, but then the wheels began to spin uselessly again. Paco put the engine back into first gear and tried to go forward this time, but nothing happened. He accelerated the engine as hard as it would go until Dani feared that he was going to damage it. If the motor packed up then they would be stranded for sure.

"Lay off a bit Paco, let's get out and see what's happened."

"Mierda!" exclaimed the driver. He turned the engine off and then he and Dani jumped out of the cab and splashed down into the mud where the road should have been. They walked around to the back where they were met with Fernando's head sticking out of the canvas.

"What's up?" he wanted to know.

"We're stuck," responded Paco with a grunt.

Fernando jumped down into the mud and together the three of them peered at the back wheels.

"There's a lot of melt water at the moment coming down from the hills and this rain hasn't helped," said Paco. "If we had been on the main road this wouldn't have happened."

"What can we do?" asked Fernando.

"We can try pushing here at the back," suggested Dani. "Give it another go Paco and we'll push." Just then it started to rain even more heavily, the rain seemed to want to push the lorry still further down into the mud and the men with it. Elizabeth's face appeared to see what was going on. "Stay inside," Dani told her. "We're going to try to push it out of the mud."

Paco was back in the cab and the engine made the whole lorry shake with the violence of its ignition.

"Okay Nando, let's give it all we've got," shouted Dani above the noise of the wind and rain. The two men leant hard against the rear of the lorry their feet submerged in water and as soon as Paco floored the accelerator they heaved with all their might. The wheels spun and muddy water flew up all over them but still they pushed for all they were worth, but it was no use. Paco stopped accelerating and came back to see them.

"It didn't move an inch," he complained. "What the hell can we do now?"

"It's too heavy that's what," said Dani. "We're never going to be able to push it out. We're going to have to take out some of the weight."

"Mierda!" cursed Paco.

"Come on, let's get cracking. Nando, you and Beth push things to the back and we'll take them down," shouted Dani. Paco returned to the cab to shut off the engine and then came back to help unload. The cans of petrol were taken off first and then a small tool box, but of course these didn't really make much difference to the lorry's overall weight.

"That's all there is apart from our kit bags and the crates," Fernando told them.

"We'll just have to start unloading crates," said Dani, "what other choice do we have. Use the torch and undo the ropes, let's start taking them off." He looked around in the darkness and realised that they were on the edge of some kind of pine forest with tall trees bordering the road to the left hand side.

The rain seemed to ease a little and no longer stung their hands and faces. They were beginning to feel the cold too, up in the mountains and soaked to the skin with a freezing wind tugging at their bedraggled uniforms. It took a while for Fernando to free the top row of crates on the driver's side of the lorry, and then he and Elizabeth pulled one down onto the floor with a thud and pushed it across to the tailgate where Dani and the driver were waiting. It was heavier than Dani had expected and it took all his strength to help Paco get it down from the lorry and place it a little further up the road out of the way. After the first crate they returned for a second. It wasn't long before they were sweating despite the chill of the night around them. After three crates they stopped for a breather and the rain intensified again as soon as they did.

"We'd better hurry up," mumbled Paco, "we're losing a lot of time." Dani nodded and they got back to work. His arm muscles were beginning to ache. His body wasn't used to this sort of hard work, and any strength he had once possessed had drained away having lived on near-starvation rations for the last two years. He was soon puffing and panting with the strain. After six crates Paco tried to extract the lorry once more, once again Fernando and Dani pushed as hard as they could but once again without any success.

"Let me take over for a while," suggested Fernando seeing that Dani was looking exhausted.

"Okay, you do a few and then Paco can have a break and I'll help you."

"I'm fine," grunted Paco.

"We've got a long drive ahead of us, so you'll need a break too," Dani informed him. The driver didn't argue with him, which was a sign that he too was finding it heavy work. The metal crates would be fairly heavy on their own, but whatever was inside them was making them almost impossible to carry, no wonder the lorry had stuck in the mud so easily. Dani climbed up into the lorry, grateful to be out of the wind and rain for a while. Now that they were on the bottom row of six crates it was an easier job just to push them across the floor to the back of the lorry.

"How many do you think we'll have to unload?" Elizabeth whispered to him as they waited for the other two to return for another load.

"Maybe all of them," said Dani.

"Then we've got to load them all on board again. If we can get the lorry free from the mud that is."

"Yes, we're losing a lot of time."

Elizabeth reached over and held his wrist for a second.

"Don't worry. It will be all right," she told him and she smiled at him although she didn't know if he could see her in the gloom, and then she let go of his wrist and wondered where she had suddenly found the inner strength to even begin to understand his burden of responsibility. The other two arrived back and hauled off another heavy crate, the last one from the driver's side of the lorry. Dani jumped back down into the muddy water and was relieved that the torrential rain of before was now dying down into just an annoying steady drizzle.

"Let's give it another go, we've got half of it out now," he told the others. "You push Paco, I'll try to drive it out." He was worried that Paco was going to wreck the engine as he was in a foul temper. Up in the cab Dani turned the ignition and gently pushed down on the accelerator. He thought for a second that the huge vehicle was going to move forward, but it didn't and so he shut off the engine and went back to help Fernando unload more of their cargo and give Paco a bit of a break.

After six more crates they tried once more, but it was clear that they were going to have to finish the job. Eventually, after a super-human effort they had emptied the back of the lorry and once again Dani started the engine. His heart was in his mouth as it fired up and he pressed gingerly down on the peddle hoping that this time it would move at last. It seemed lighter now, almost as if it was ready to escape from the mud, but infuriatingly it still didn't quite make it. Dani turned off the engine once again and sat with his head in his hands for a second wondering if there was anything else left to try. If they were stuck here for the night then they would probably be overrun by the advancing rebels the next day. Their situation was perilous.

At the back of the lorry he found Fernando and Paco with their hands on their hips, worry written across their tired mud-splattered faces.

"It almost moved," Fernando informed him, "it's just the wheels keep slipping back."

Dani looked around them in the darkness hoping for inspiration, and seeing the tall pine trees he found it.

"Let's cut some pine branches and lay them by the wheels, maybe the needles will give us a bit of traction," he suggested.

"It might work," agreed Paco. He went over to the tool box and found a knife and then with Fernando he disappeared a little way into the forest looking for low hanging branches.

"I should help push too," said Elizabeth. Dani was about to tell her that she should stay in the lorry and not get wet and muddy, but he sort of sensed that it was important for her to be able to help.

"Can you drive?" he asked her.

"No."

"Well, don't worry, it's not too difficult, I'll show you what to do. With the three of us pushing and the pine needles giving a bit of traction it might just come out."

"What if it doesn't?"

"Then we'll have to go looking for some help. There might be a farm around here with some horses, or at least a couple of extra men to help push."

"Will they help us?"

"Sure, we're all still Republicans Comrade Nurse, things might not be going too well, but people don't forget which side they're on."

The other two men reappeared out of the forest with armfuls of branches covered in long thin needles. Dani helped place them under all the wheels and then he took Elizabeth to the cab and started the engine. Then he climbed out of the driver's side door to allow her to take her place at the wheel.

"Right, push your left foot down on the left hand pedal, all the way to the floor." Elizabeth tried and found it a lot harder than she would have imagined.

"I can't do it," she complained.

"Yes you can. Push harder." She tried harder and at last the pedal moved downwards.

"I've done it!" she shrieked excitedly.

"Good. Now when I shout to you, push down with your right foot on the right hand pedal, but gently, and as you do so, let the left hand pedal come up slightly. The lorry should move forward then."

"What should I do if it does move?" she asked breathless at the effort of holding down the clutch pedal with her small foot.

"Just keep it moving as long as you can, I'll come and help you then. Ready?"

"Ready." He patted her arm and shut the door. Once he was at the back of the lorry with the other two he shouted out to her to start to accelerate. The three men heaved with all their might. It was now or never, their whole mission depended on them getting the lorry out of its muddy grave. Suddenly the lorry started to move, the wheels found purchase on the carpet of pine needles and the lorry surged forward and then stalled. But it was enough. Paco was in the cab instantly restarting the motor and the lorry crawled forward a little more. Dani and Fernando pushed hard one last time and finally it was clear of the muddy area at the bottom of the slope.

Paco pulled on the handbrake and they set about the task of reloading the heavy cargo. It was harder work to lift the crates up than it had been to take them down, but their spirits were high at having succeeded in freeing their vehicle and saving their mission. They sweated despite the cold, and their muscles ached, but eventually they had everything back inside. Dani knew they had lost a lot of time, but at least they were able to move on again.

They set off as soon as the last crate was safely stowed leaving Fernando and Elizabeth huddled up in blankets in the back. Dani and the driver sat in the cab with their clothes steaming in the heat. The driver produced a crumpled packet of cigarettes from under his cape and offered it to Dani. The Captain refused. Paco fumbled for some matches and when he found them Dani lit one for him so that he could still concentrate on the road ahead. They'd had enough excitement already without driving off the road into a ditch all for the sake of a cigarette. Dani had never smoked, since his father always started to cough and splutter whenever anyone lit up near him, he said his lungs just couldn't stand it. The cab filled with the smell of beech smoke.

The road climbed slowly through the pine forest, the dark trees reaching out to touch the lorry as if to try to hold it back. The rain had stopped at last and the storm had moved away somewhere else and a weak moon was just visible through the sombre clouds. It was an eerie place and Dani would be glad when they were back in more open country.

"Maybe we could use the main road for a bit and make up some lost time," suggested Paco after a while.

"I guess so," Dani decided, "but we'll have to be well away from it by dawn." The main Valencia Highroad had been the Republic's thin umbilical cord for most of the war, linking the besieged capital to the port of Valencia where the government had fled when it seemed that Madrid might fall. Now the cord had been cut. Dani was worried that the Rebels might have surged down the highway out of Madrid and somehow be ahead of them. Still, if they spent the rest of the night meandering up and down through these hills then they weren't going to get very far at all. It was a risk to travel on the main road, but it was a risk they had to take.

The lorry descended down into another valley and they reached the town of Perales. The streets were deserted, but the collection of tiny houses looked as if they had been abandoned years ago. Just beyond the town, crossing the bridge over the Tajuña River they were able to link up with the main highway. They saw people again. Some were huddled in small family groups at the side of the road trying to get some rest under the trees, others were still walking, taking advantage of the improved weather conditions. Those who heard the lorry approaching turned to stare at it as it loomed out of the darkness, wondering where it had suddenly come from and to which side it might belong. You could see the relief on their faces when the realised that it was an ambulance. And then the cries for help would start.

The refugees meant that they had to travel at a reduced speed, but it was better than the narrow winding roads of before. They were climbing again through the hills, the lorry's great engine struggling with the load. It was all that Dani could do in his exhausted state to keep awake and so he opened the window a little to allow in some of the chill from outside.

"This is better," said the driver. "Now we're making some progress at last." Dani smiled and nodded in agreement, but he was worried about being on the main highway when he had been told to avoid it.

They passed through another small town at the top of the rise and then began to descend towards the River Tajo down in the valley beneath them. As they came around a bend just on the outskirts of the village of Fuentidueña de Tajo they saw a road block up ahead of them. There were two soldiers in the road, obviously alerted by the sound of an approaching motor vehicle.

"Dios!" exclaimed Dani when he saw what was ahead and he instinctively reached to touch his pistol just to reassure himself that it was where it should be. There was no way they could turn back now without arising the soldiers' suspicions. Dani felt his whole body tense with nervous excitement as Paco began to slow the lorry as they approached the soldiers.

FIVE

As they got closer to the soldiers Dani was surprised to see how young they were. Their tattered uniforms gave them away as Republican soldiers, but it didn't mean that they were still loyal to the cause. They might be waiting to welcome the first of the advancing Rebels in order to surrender their town. Both soldiers had their rifles in their hands pointing vaguely in the driver's direction. The lorry stopped.

One of the soldiers approached Dani's door the other stayed firmly in the middle of the road. Dani wound down his window.

"Buenas Noches, comrade," said Dani.

"I need to see some papers Comrade Captain," stated the young soldier his face pale in the difficult light.

"We're taking a wounded soldier to Albacete," Dani informed him and carefully reached inside his jacket to get the General's orders. He did it slowly so as not to cause alarm and extracted the folded piece of paper from beneath his cape. He passed it out to the waiting soldier. The young guard pulled a small torch from his pocket and set about reading the orders, his face lined with concentration within his woollen balaclava.

"So you've come from Madrid?" asked the soldier after a while.

"Yes comrade, we got out just in time."

"Are the Rebels far behind you?"

"I don't know. Not far I shouldn't think. I expect they'll be here tomorrow." A look of panic came over the soldier's face. It must have suddenly occurred to him that the next lorry to appear around the bend might belong to the enemy.

"My orders are to search all motor vehicles for deserters," he stated. "I need to look in the back."

"If you must," agreed Dani who was starting to get irritated at the delay.

Dani got out of the cab and accompanied the guard around to the back of the lorry. He pulled back the canvas to allow the other man to see inside. The soldier shone his torch inside and could just make out the faces of the two people there wrapped in heavy blankets. He was surprised to see a woman despite the fact that it was an ambulance.

"I need you to get out," he told them. Fernando looked at Dani who nodded and then he climbed down from the tailgate. He reached up a hand to help the English nurse.

The young soldier called out to his companion to cover them while he went inside, he leant his rifle against the back of the lorry. It didn't take him long to lift a tarpaulin sheet and find their secret cargo.

"What's in these containers?" he wanted to know.

"Nothing much, just medical supplies, nothing for you to worry about comrade," said Dani.

"I need to open one," decided the soldier touching a padlock with shaking fingers.

"Okay. Let me help you," said Dani. The Captain climbed up into the back of the lorry and as he did so he withdrew his pistol and shoved it into the young soldier's face.

"Listen here comrade," whispered Dani, "we're on a very important mission for the Republic and your delaying us is making me very angry. I can't let you open a container, no-one is to open one, do you understand? My orders are to shoot anyone who tries."

"I understand," stammered the guard, terrified of what might happen to him.

"Good, now we're going to get down and you're going to tell your mate that everything is in order and then you're going to let us through. If you don't cooperate we'll kill you both."

Suddenly, a shot rang out. Dani saw a look of pure panic on the young soldier's face as he realised that he had left his rifle down at the back of the lorry. He made a scramble for it, but Dani pushed him down and kept the pistol in his face.

"Nando, what's happening?" he shouted.

"That idiot Paco just shot the other guard."

"Fuck!" Dani exclaimed. He hauled the terrified soldier with him down out of the lorry despite his whimpering protests and threw him on the ground. Elizabeth was kneeling over the body of the guard who had been shot and Paco stood over her, revolver in hand.

"Why did you shoot him?" Dani demanded.

"Because we're wasting time here. It'll be dawn soon if we don't get a move on."

"He's just a boy," whispered Elizabeth trying not to cry. Seeing that they were distracted the other young soldier decided to make a run for it, he leapt up and ducked along the other side of the lorry and set off down an embankment running for his life. Paco, Dani and Fernando ran after him but he was already getting away. Paco raised his gun and fired away into the darkness the sound of the shot ringing out clearly into the night.

"Will you stop shooting," shouted Dani.

"We can't just let him get away," protested Paco raising his gun for another try. Dani knocked the weapon from his hand. By the time Paco had scrambled to pick up his gun the boy soldier had been swallowed up by the darkness.

"Now look what you've done," shouted Paco, his face red with rage. "He'll sound the alarm and we'll have the whole local army out against us."

"I think your shooting has already woken the whole town anyway, don't forget that those kids were on our side."

"Our side today their side tomorrow, what's the difference," grumbled the driver.

"Let's get going as quickly as we can before the militia come," decided Dani. Let's break down that barricade Nando."

Fernando pulled his arm out from his sling and set off after Dani. He was a bit reluctant to turn his back on Paco, but Dani seemed to be unafraid. The barricade was made up of broken furniture and there were two metal bedsteads in the middle which were obviously intended to serve as a gateway. They threw the bedsteads to the side of the road and Paco drove the lorry through. Just for a second it appeared that he might drive on past and leave them behind, but then he slammed on the brakes and the lorry ground to a halt in the gravel.

"Elizabeth, come on," shouted Dani seeing the nurse still kneeling beside the bleeding boy soldier. She was cradling his head in her hands holding it up from the mud of the track. She seemed not to hear Dani. He walked across to her. As he arrived in the strange hellish glow of the lorry's taillights he saw the young man's eyelids flicker and then his eyes rolled back and he was gone. He watched as Elizabeth gently laid his head on the ground.

"We've got to go," whispered Dani, "I'm sorry about that." Elizabeth wiped a tear from the corner of her eye and stood up. She looked at Dani her face contorted with sadness and then brushed past him to climb up into the lorry. Fernando reached down to help her. Dani returned to the cab and they set off down the slope towards the village itself. He could only hope that anyone who had heard the shooting would assume that the Rebels had arrived and that it was safer to stay indoors. What he didn't need was a local militia intent on trying to go out in a blaze of irrelevant glory.

Out of the darkness loomed the ruins of a castle tower perched on a small hill overlooking the village, and beyond, visible in the patchy moonlight, was a church around which were clustered some low stone houses. As they neared the centre they saw a group of men with rifles gathering together outside the town hall in the main square. On seeing the lorry the group started to run towards them.

"Let's get the hell out of here," shouted Dani at Paco, but the driver had already floored the accelerator and the lorry lurched forward in response. The sound of a rifle being fired rang out. The lorry roared through the narrow confines of the main streets between the tightly-packed houses and hurtled at top speed down towards the bridge across the River Tajo. It was a long iron bridge spanning the wide river and Dani hoped that there were no guards there.

Paco slowed the lorry as they came up to the bridge and without warning a sentry stepped out of the shadows and levelled his rifle at them.

"Don't stop," shouted Dani at the driver, but Paco had already worked that one out for himself and pushed his foot down hard. The two men in the cab ducked instinctively in case there was a shot. There was a loud thud and then the front left wheel rode up over something and the lorry veered to the side and slammed into the first support of the iron bridge. Had Dani not been crouched down he might have been thrown through the windscreen, as it was he had just hit his head on the dashboard. He was dazed and felt a trickle of blood running down his forehead. He reached up and touched it and then sat looking at the blood on his fingers.

Fernando came round to Dani's side of the cab and pulled open the door.

"What happened? Are you all right?"

"I'm okay. A sentry stepped out on us. What happened to Paco?" They both looked across at the driver who was slumped forward over the wheel. There was a crack in the windscreen smeared with blood where he must have hit his head. The motor was still running, complaining of something, but still running.

"Let's get him into the back, I'll drive," decided Fernando quickly. They hauled him across and out of Dani's side of the cab since the other door was jammed up against the bridge support. They were just heaving the unconscious Paco up into the back of the lorry when they heard shouts coming from behind them. The armed militia was after them.

"Oh shit!" Exclaimed Fernando and he raced back to the cab. A bullet pinged off the iron of the bridge slightly away to his right. In the back Elizabeth was helping Dani get Paco fully onboard when they heard the first shot. Dani left what he was doing and drew his revolver. It was too late now to try to convince the villagers that they were on the same side.

*

Captain Roberto Ruiz Roman lay awake in his bed waiting for it to be nearly dawn so that he could head back to the airbase and get ten planes up at first light. He wasn't a good sleeper at the best of times. He suffered terribly from nightmares and usually in order to get any kind of rest at all he had to wipe himself out with drink. He preferred expensive scotch but in a war it wasn't easy to come by, so he made do with whatever terrible brandy had been captured from the enemy. As the war dragged on and the Republic's situation became more and more desperate, so the quality of the brandy got worse and worse.

But not tonight, he wasn't bothered about sleeping and therefore he didn't need a drink. There must be some good stuff too somewhere in Madrid, hidden away. Roberto was good at sniffing out Reds, but not so good at sniffing out fine scotch, but others were and they knew he was ready to pay good money for the real thing. He had nothing to spend his money on except drink. He didn't play cards and he didn't go with whores, he felt they were beneath him. In most of the captured towns and cities there was usually a woman ready to throw herself at him, perhaps to save the life of a husband or sweetheart. Roberto listened to the problems of these women, agreed that he might possibly be able to help them in some unspecified way, took advantage of their gratitude and then did nothing whatsoever for them. He had normally moved on somewhere new by the time their husband or lover had been shot.

He couldn't for the life of him work out why he suffered from nightmares. It wasn't that he felt guilty for what he did, no way, it was his job to get information out of people and he enjoyed it, so it was strange that his mind was storing up images of the people he tortured and killed to play back to him in sleep. Perhaps the nightmares would go away now that the war was over, if not he would just have to continue to drink himself into oblivion whenever he needed to sleep.

Roberto lay on his bed listening to a clock tick. He knew it hadn't been more than five minutes since he had last checked the time, so he resisted the urge to look again. From outside the door of his room came the muffled snores of his driver who was asleep in the corridor, ready to leave at a moment's notice. As soon as he had his ten planes up searching, he had decided that he would set off along the Valencia Highroad. It should be safe by the morning as the advanced units had already set out from Madrid the previous evening. Soon they would reach Valencia and Alicante and the Republic would be totally wiped off the map. He was sad in a way that the war was about to come to an end, still, he had this one last great mission to deal with and he was determined to enjoy it. Afterwards, he would find some interesting way to serve the Nationalist cause. Any new regime would have its enemies and of course there were many traitors from the Republican army still to be dealt with. The future didn't look so bad. Damn why was this night lasting such a long time?

SIX

Dani fired out of the back of the lorry above the heads of the onrushing mob. He didn't want to have to kill anyone. They were just simple folk protecting their village against a supposed enemy. The shot had the desired effect, making the militia hesitate. It was now in the mind of each and every one of them that they were up against real soldiers and that it was very likely that some of them would die. They hesitated, waiting for a leader to emerge from amongst them, waiting for a volunteer to take the first bullet. This was time enough for Fernando to put the lorry into reverse pull back a bit to get clearance of the bridge support and then they were beginning to cross. Seeing them fleeing renewed the militia's vigour and they rushed after them once more. A shot rang out and a bullet whipped through the canvas.

"Get down," Dani shouted behind him to Elizabeth and she crouched low at the back of the lorry invisible in the darkness. It was then that Dani remembered the sticks of dynamite that were also there.

"Pass me one of the sticks of dynamite," he instructed the nurse. She fumbled around in the dark and eventually her hand touched one and she passed it forward to him. Dani had never used dynamite before but he knew it had been a popular weapon with the miners of Asturias when they were defending their homeland. There was a fuse coming out of one end which he knew he would have to light. He panicked for a moment as he had no matches, and then he remembered that Paco had been smoking before. He rummaged around in Paco's jacket pockets until he found what he was looking for.

With shaking fingers and with the bouncing motion of the lorry as it crossed the long bridge it was not easy for Dani to strike a match, but at the third attempt he managed it. Elizabeth saw the bright burst of light and saw Dani touch it to the fuse. As soon as the fuse caught he tossed the stick of dynamite out of the back of the lorry onto the bridge. There was a short delay and then an almighty explosion. The force of the blast knocked Dani over and he fell to the back of the lorry and landed on top of Elizabeth who was still crouching there. He clumsily managed to get to his feet once more.

"Sorry about that," he said to her. He couldn't see her face but he hoped she wasn't angry. He moved back to the lorry's tailgate and looked out to see what the dynamite had done. There was a twisted black hole in the floor of the bridge and some of the metal at the sides was bent out of shape. The militia had stopped in their tracks to gape at the damage with all thoughts of pursuing the ambulance now gone. Dani wondered what they would do when the real enemy arrived in the next few hours. The best thing they could do would be to run to the hills, since the first thing the Rebels would do would be to shoot anyone who had been part of a militia, and there would be plenty of villagers willing to give out the names of those involved in order to guarantee their own safety.

Once over the bridge, they began to climb up out of the valley, the lorry's motor snarling angrily. Fernando drove carefully, trying not to ask too much of the straining engine as it laboured to keep them going. Paco was beginning to make moaning noises, and soon his eyelids began to flutter as he started to regain consciousness. As soon as the road levelled out a bit Dani banged on the cab wall to get Fernando to stop and leaving Paco in Elizabeth's capable hands he went to inspect the damage at the front of the lorry with his friend. The two ugly metal bars at the front had done their job of protecting the engine and even the headlight on the driver's side was still working although the glass was cracked, but the worrying thing was a long piece of metal that had speared itself through the radiator grill and was firmly lodged inside. Dani reached over with his hand and touched it. He tried to move it but it was stuck fast.

"Can you pull it out?" asked Fernando.

"I don't think so," replied the captain, "maybe we should just leave it there, it's still running after all, if we mess with it we might make matters worse. Perhaps Paco can take a look at it when we rest up for the day."

"How is he?"

"He was just starting to regain consciousness when we stopped."

"So he's going to be all right?"

"I don't know, Beth will tell us later. Right now we had better keep going for as long as we can. There can't be much darkness left now and a dynamited bridge isn't going to hold up the whole Rebel army for very long."

"Do you really think that they are that close behind us?"

"I don't know amigo, but they could be. So let's put as much distance as we can between us and them before we have to find somewhere to hide up." They climbed up into the cab and set off once more. The engine continued to complain but it continued to work and so they made slow but steady progress always upwards through the hills. As soon as they could they turned off the main road and took an unmade track to skirt around Tarancón which was the next place on their route. Dani didn't want to risk running across another roadblock or driving through the centre of another village.

*

Captain Roberto Ruiz Roman sprang out of bed, he could stand it no longer. It had been the longest night of his life and he couldn't put up with a minute more of inactivity. He was a hunter of Reds and so he needed to be up hunting Reds not lying in bed unable to sleep. He opened the door of his room and found his driver lying curled up like a baby on the tiled floor of the corridor outside. He kicked him savagely in the ribs and the man groaned and sat up rubbing his eyes.

"Let's go. We've got a million things to do today. It's going to be a great day, I can feel it," said the Captain. The driver followed him out of the small pensión where they had spent the night and then raced ahead to get the staff car started. He realised when he had the car running that he would need headlights because it was still dark. He was a tough bastard this one, never thought of anything except finding Reds. The driver wondered how long it would be before he could ask for a transfer to something saner without the Captain having him shot. Or maybe today really would be a great day and someone would put a bullet through the Captain's brain.

They hurtled at full speed towards the airport, it was the only way the driver knew how to drive and that suited Roberto just fine. Once they arrived at Cuatro Vientos, the captain went to find his ten pilots and the driver curled up in a ball in the back of the staff car and went back to dreaming about his girl back in Burgos.

Not surprisingly the pilots were still asleep. They had been flying missions almost non-stop for weeks in the build up of pressure on the Spanish capital, and now that Madrid had finally capitulated they had

40

been expecting a little less flying time. Then here comes some pompous-arsed little captain who reckons he's Franco himself, dishing out orders left right and centre and suddenly they're being woken at six again.

By seven, just as the sun was beginning to think about putting in an appearance the ten planes started their engines and prepared for takeoff. The captain had told them that they were looking for a big lorry trying to make its way along the Valencia highroad. He put them into pairs and gave each pair a section of the highway to patrol. The lorry might not actually be travelling by day he had said, so they would need to check out any possible hiding places near to the road.

As soon as the planes were airborne Roberto woke his driver and sent him to look for petrol. Once they had a full tank they could set off along the Valencia road themselves. He had a motorcycle courier standing by at the airport to come and find him if there was any news from the planes. Communications were a real headache moving out into the recently-captured zones and he wanted the motorcycle as backup in case the phone lines were down.

*

They skirted around the town of Tarancón where the militia might have been bigger, better led and more determined. These were desperate times and everyone was on edge. It wasn't long before they began to make out the first signs of the approaching dawn, just a brief hint of red away between the peaks of the sierras.

"Let's start thinking of somewhere to hide up for the day," Dani instructed Fernando. It wasn't going to be easy to find a suitable place since they were no longer surrounded by pine forests. Here it was open hillside and scrubland. Had they passed by a month earlier they would have found the whole area still under snow, but now in the last days of March the snow had melted away into the nearby reservoirs and the daytime temperatures were starting to increase. It was still cold at night though. At the moment the fields were green with new shoots, but when the heat of the summer kicked in, it soon became brown and parched. There were no tall trees, just a few dwarf bushes dotted about.

Unexpectedly, Dani found himself thinking about the sea. When you were brought up living beside the Mediterranean you couldn't imagine that there were places like this, the Mancha Alta, where the majority of

41

people had never seen the sea. For a moment he let his tired mind wander back to his childhood and the long walks he used to take with his father along the beach in the late winter afternoons when his father had finished teaching for the day. His father was a shy man really, especially when compared to the Spaniards who surrounded him, but alone with his son, speaking his own language rather than fumbling in Castellano, he talked and talked. Dani would ask him about this strange place called England whose language his father insisted on him speaking even though he had never been there. And his father would tell him about the beautiful cherry orchards of his youth, the fields of swaying wheat, the tiny hidden villages clustered around pointed churches and Dani would look out across the gentle blue of the Mediterranean and wonder how far across the water he would have to go to get there. His father had always promised him that one day he would take him and his mother there.

Crossing a stone bridge over a melt-water stream Fernando noticed a small lake across the fields in the distance. Down towards the lake was a grey-walled farm. It must have been abandoned for some time because most of the farmhouse roof was missing, blown away by the winter storms that liked to patrol the sierras. What interested Fernando though was an old outbuilding which seemed tall enough to be able to hide the lorry. He pointed this out to Dani who soon agreed that they ought to investigate. Turning off the road they started to bump along the track towards the lake.

"I don't want to alarm you Dani," said Fernando, "but I think there's smoke coming out of the engine." The captain peered forward and saw that what his friend said was indeed true. A thin plume of smoke was rising up from the front of the lorry, visible now that the day was beginning to break.

"Looks like we don't have a choice," Dani decided, "this farm will have to do. Let's hope that Paco can fix the engine."

"Let's hope that English nurse knows her stuff and can fix Paco," said Fernando.

The track dipped sharply down and then there was a slow steady climb up towards the farm house. It was a desolate place. It would have been cut off through the winter, at the mercy of the cold winds sweeping down from the mountains, drifting the snow around the walls, and then bleached by the sun in the summer. The only time it would have been any good for farming would have been the spring and the autumn. This was an area for early cereal crops and late vegetables and goats that could somehow survive, where other animals would have perished. The freshwater lake was without doubt the reason for someone deciding to farm there, but even that had not been enough to keep the farm alive. Or maybe the old folk had died and their sons had been killed at some distant front called Guadalajara or Aragón.

Fernando slowed the lorry to a crawl, as they got near to the first scattered outbuildings of the farm, and the plume of smoke from the motor got thicker. Dani drew his revolver from its holster. There didn't appear to be anyone around, but he wasn't about to leave anything to chance.

"Stop here and let's go check the place out shall we," said Dani. Fernando brought the lorry to a gentle halt and they climbed down from the cab. Fernando also brought out his pistol. They paused briefly to look at the smoking radiator and then, cautiously, they walked forward towards the farm house and the big stone barn. Their ears were straining to catch the slightest sound that might be out of place, but for the moment there was only the gentle lap of the water of the nearby lake, caught by the early morning breeze. They checked the high-walled barn first and found it suitable to hide away the lorry and then went through the rotten farmhouse door and looked around inside. It was obvious that no-one had set foot in there for a generation. There were a few items of broken furniture and Dani half expected to find a dead body or two, but in the end the house was completely empty. Maybe the lake had flooded one year and the owners had abandoned the place.

They went back to the lorry and found Elizabeth waiting for them, the sun rising behind her giving her auburn hair a glow like fire.

"Are we going to stop here?" she asked.

"Yes, it seems all right," said Dani, "we can put the lorry inside the barn as long as we cover it over a bit because a lot of the roof is missing. How's Paco doing?"

"He's sleeping at the moment, but I need to keep a close eye on him. He had a nasty blow to the head and he might well have concussion. Why is there smoke coming out of the engine?"

"There's a piece of metal sticking out of it. We're hoping that Paco will be able to take a look at it when he wakes up."

"It doesn't look good," Elizabeth told him. Dani shrugged. What could he say? No, it didn't look good, that was obvious. Did she want him to lie to her and say that it was nothing and that they'd soon be able to fix it, or did she want the truth that if the engine packed up then they would be stranded in this godforsaken place until the Rebels came to liberate it. They still had a stick of dynamite left and they would have to blow up the lorry and its secret cargo and maybe it would be for the best for them to be inside the lorry too.

Dani and Fernando worked in the barn clearing a space big enough for the lorry, throwing out some of the fallen rafters from the roof and then Fernando started up the motor once more. The smoke had never stopped slowly funnelling skywards from the radiator, but when the engine was restarted it got thicker and blacker. There was nothing they could do, they couldn't leave it out in the open. The big red crosses on the roof and sides would have been visible to an enemy plane from miles away. Dani held open the one remaining barn door as Fernando drove in, and then his friend quickly cut the engine to save it from further damage. They stood and looked at it for a while hoping that it wouldn't catch fire.

SEVEN

Once they were satisfied that the engine was not about to explode into flames, they placed some broken planks over the roof of the lorry to keep it hidden from nosey aircraft and then Dani and Fernando walked over to the lake. Their uniforms were still damp from being soaked during the night, despite the waterproof capes they had been wearing. Like any good soldiers they were not going to pass up the chance to have a wash and a bathe, they never knew when their next opportunity might be. After taking off their boots, they walked slowly out into the lake, the freezing melt water taking their breath away as they got deeper. Dani turned to look at his friend who was just behind him and Fernando gave a quick laugh and threw himself into the water. Dani did the same and they both came up for air gasping with the cold. They laughed and splashed each other like kids, but the water here was not the warm joy of their Mediterranean childhoods and they soon waded out of the lake once more. They stripped off their tatty uniforms, which at least were clean of all the mud from their work in the night, and laid them on the grass to dry. Then they slumped down to rest, shivering in the weak early morning sun.

Dani closed his eyes and let his mind relax as much as he could. His head ached a bit from where he had smashed into the dashboard when they had hit the bridge, but at least he had been able to clean off the dried blood from his forehead. There was a tiny gash, nothing more and a slight ache, but he felt okay. The headache might even be as a result of the problem with the lorry's motor which was uppermost in his mind. When Paco had rested he would be able to look at it, although there was no hope of getting any spares of course.

Elizabeth, satisfied that Paco was resting quietly, left the barn to look for the other two. She saw them over by the lake and was just about to go over and have a wash herself when she realised that they had taken off their uniforms and were in just their underwear. She would have to leave it until later. Instead she went into the farmhouse to see if there was anything of interest there. She was struck by how simple the inside was, just a few minimal bits of broken furniture and a small bedroom. It must have been a desolate place to live out here by the lake, alone throughout the long winter months, trapped by the snow. She thought she would probably have gone mad. Perhaps that was why the place was empty now, the farmer had gone crazy during one long winter night and butchered his family before shooting himself with his hunting rifle. She shivered at the thought and went back outside. She sat down on the low stone wall of the pigsty and waited for the other two to come back from the lake. She could hear her patient snoring, but louder still was her stomach grumbling about the lack of breakfast. She had hoped that there might be something in the farmhouse, a big loaf of warm bread, a jar of olive oil and a hanging leg of cured ham would have been nice, anything would have been nice. She had never known such an acute hunger as she had been feeling over the last few hours and she wondered if the men had any more food hidden away. Soldiers always had something to eat, didn't they? At the hospital the soldiers who were well enough to be able to go out for a few hours always seemed to come back with something extra. Usually it was a bottle of some dubious home-brewed alcohol that did no-one any good, but sometimes it would be some cheese or a chorizo. They always shared their spoils with everyone, including her, especially her. She knew a lot of the young men in her care had crushes on her. She had had more marriage proposals from wounded men than she could remember. At first she had been embarrassed and taken them seriously and felt really bad about telling the men that she couldn't accept, but she had soon learned to just laugh off such proposals, just as the other nurses did.

Seeing as the other two didn't appear to be in any hurry to return, she began to take out the pins from her hair and let her auburn tresses tumble free for the first time since she had left her quarters at the military hospital. She decided she would wash her hair and uniform in the lake like the men when they were finished. She would have to hope that they wouldn't look at her. She would never normally have considered doing such a thing, but these were exceptional circumstances and she didn't know how long it would be, before she might be able to get a proper bath. She found herself wondering what they might find if they managed to reach Alicante. It seemed that everyone was heading south and hoping that there would be ships at the ports of Valencia, Cartagena and Alicante to take them to safety. Elizabeth wasn't convinced that the Republic had any friends remaining who might wish to help with the evacuation of thousands of defeated people. In Madrid the question that people most wanted to ask her was why hadn't Britain come to the Republic's aid? Of course she hadn't known the answer, but she doubted that Britain would get involved now that it was all over. And she worried for her personal safety. What would the victorious do with the women of the vanquished? What would they do to a foreign woman who had come to help the enemy. She shuddered and preferred to think about washing her hair and uniform and lying on the grass by the lake as the men were doing drying slowly in the morning sun.

She heard a noise from the barn and saw that Paco had emerged from the lorry. He was holding one hand against his head, feeling the bandages that she had used in the night to cover a nasty cut on his forehead.

"Paco. How do you feel?" she called out to him.

"I feel like shit," he replied and then he went on some rambling speech cursing everyone he could think of who might in any way be responsible for his pain, but Elizabeth didn't understand most of it.

"Where's the Captain?" he asked her eventually when he had calmed down. She pointed over towards the lake and watched as Paco stumbled across the farmyard to get to the others. She wanted to ask him about the food situation, but she held her tongue. She would have to wait until the men had finished at the lake. She almost wished that she hadn't shared her bar of chocolate the previous day, she would quite happily have eaten it all by herself right then and there. God she had to stop thinking about food.

*

Captain Roberto Ruiz Roman took a big bite of the loaf of bread he had got from the airforce field kitchen. There was some sort of stew on offer, possibly goat, but it smelt rancid and so he just had bread and a mug of what passed for coffee but in reality could have been anything dirty-brown to colour the water. At least it was warm. He was sitting at a wooden table, still waiting for his driver to come back with a full tank of petrol and a couple of spare cans to make sure they had enough for any eventualities. He didn't know where the man had gone to get petrol in Madrid, but his driver was normally pretty good at getting what the captain needed. There must be Nationalist tankers already in the capital in order for the troop carriers and tanks to refuel for the push south. The driver had taken Roberto's orders which said they were to receive every possible assistance for their mission without question.

There was no news so far from the ten planes he had sent up. If only he had been a pilot then he would have been up there himself looking. He would fly the whole length of the Valencia Highroad if he had to. He heard the sound of an approaching car and looked up to see his driver and the little black staff car. At last he could set off. As soon as the driver stopped Roberto opened the passenger side door and jumped in.

"Don't I get the chance to have a little breakfast Captain?" moaned the driver.

"Here," said Roberto tossing the half eaten loaf into his lap, "you can eat it while you drive. What took you so long?"

*

At last the men came back from the lake. They had been there most of the morning, resting, letting their uniforms dry, just trying to relax after the excitement of their night's work. Their clothes were still damp, but at least they felt clean. They found the English nurse curled up asleep by the wall of the pigsty. She had let her hair down and all three stared at her for a moment, not wanting to wake her, but then Dani gave a gentle cough and she opened her eyes.

"You're back then," she said rubbing her face. "I was waiting to be able to have a wash."

"It's all yours," Dani told her. She stood up a bit unsteadily and noticed the three men staring at her.

"Is there anything to eat?" she asked. Fernando and Paco rushed off to find their kitbags in the back of the lorry, whilst Dani just stood there looking at the nurse. With her hair down and the sun behind her reflecting off the surface of the lake she had to be the most beautiful thing he had ever seen. His father had always told him that English women were beautiful, but never in the presence of his mother of course. Fernando came back first, offering Elizabeth the final third of a small loaf of bread known as *pan negro* because of its dark colour. It wasn't fresh by any means, but it was just about still edible. Paco returned with a tin which he opened with his knife to reveal some tiny sardines. From his pocket he produced his final and best offering with a little magician's

48

flourish, a small can of condensed milk. He jabbed a couple of holes through the lid with his knife and offered it to the nurse. Elizabeth looked at the three men who were watching her intently as if she were a small baby about to take its first taste of anything other than breast milk. She raised the can to her lips and tipped it slightly to get a taste of the rich contents. It was like a star exploding on her tongue, a small taste of paradise. She closed her eyes for a second letting the sensation course through her whole body and when she opened them she saw the three men smiling at her.

"Not bad huh!" said Paco.

"Delicioso," she stated and offered the can to Fernando.

"It's for you," he replied.

"Dani, I want us to share everything okay," she said in English. "If you three don't eat then I don't eat." Dani translated and so Paco got his mess tin and poured the condensed milk into it, then he carefully broke up the bread into four bite-sized pieces and dropped them into the thick creamy liquid. With his knife he offered a sardine to Elizabeth. She plucked it off the knife and stuffed it into her mouth as quickly as she could, not wanting to lose even a few drops of oil. The taste reminded her of the sea and therefore of her coastal home. As soon as the sardine had disintegrated in her mouth she helped herself to a piece of the milk-soaked bread. Licking her fingers she saw the others eating too. It wasn't the biggest breakfast ever eaten, but for her it was one she would never be able to forget.

"I need to have a wash," she said to Dani.

"Sure, the water's lovely," he lied. "We're going to have a look at the motor."

Elizabeth went to the lorry and got a small piece of greenish soap and her washcloth. Men in a war always had some secret reserve of food she thought, but women in a war always had some secret personal hygiene products hidden away. She felt guilty that she hadn't offered her soap to the men since they had been so generous with their food, but there wasn't enough for four anyway.

When she reached the edge of the water she looked back at the farmhouse to see if the men were watching her. They were nowhere in sight and she assumed that they had already started work on the wounded engine. She hoped with all her heart that they would be able to fix it. She couldn't bear to imagine dying here in this desolate, godforsaken place. She took off her cape letting it fall on the grass and then untied her white apron. She stole a final nervous glance back at the farmhouse and satisfied that no-one was looking she pulled her black woollen dress over her head and dropped it at her side. Slipping off her shoes she waded into the water soap in hand. She knew that Dani had lied about the water being nice, but she wasn't prepared for it to be quite this cold. It took her breath away. The last time she had had the luxury of a shower back in the hospital in Madrid the water hadn't been hot, but this could only just be above freezing. She felt that if she stayed in the lake for too much longer she would turn to ice. Quickly, she dipped the soap in the water and then worked up a lather on her cloth which she rushed across her face and then up and down her arms. Although she got goose bumps, it felt good to be able to get clean.

The three men had removed the engine cover and were examining the piece of metal that was sticking out of the radiator. It was obvious that water had leaked out of the radiator and that it had run dry and begun to overheat, hence the smoke. If they had driven much further the engine would have caught fire for sure.

"We need to fill it with water again and see where the leaks are," Paco decided.

"I'll go to the lake and get some," said Dani, "I'll fill our water bottles too, who knows when we'll get another chance like this." He went to the lorry to get the empty water bottles from the back and walked over to the hole in the wall by the pigsty which was their way to the lake. As he got there he froze at the sight of Elizabeth washing herself. He stood for a second, paralysed, and then decided he would have to wait until she was finished. As he turned around he heard a distant grumble from away in the sky. He knew instantly that it was an approaching aeroplane.

EIGHT

"Oh Christ," shouted Fernando who had heard the plane at the same time. He ran from the barn over to where Dani was by the gap in the wall.

"We've got to get her," he shouted as he neared his friend. Dani dropped the water bottles and they raced together across the uneven grass towards the lake.

"Elizabeth, come out of the water," Dani called out to her. She hadn't heard the plane, her ears were not as finely-tuned to the sound of approaching enemy aircraft as men who had spent time at the front, and she panicked to see the two soldiers running in her direction. She screamed and tried to run out into deeper water, tripped and fell with an ungraceful splash. She sat up in the lake spitting water out of her mouth, shocked by how easily the cold penetrated through her thin undergarments.

Dani and Fernando reached her together and quickly grabbed Elizabeth's arms to drag her upright. Shocked by their behaviour and given her state of undress she struggled against her would-be rescuers with all her might. She tugged her arm free from Dani and shoved him over into the water and then tried to do the same to Fernando.

"Un avión," Fernando informed her as clearly as he could, trying not to yell at her.

"Oh my God," she gasped. Dani re-emerged from the icy water and grabbing the arm he had briefly held before, he helped Fernando to lead her out of the lake. As the water got shallower so they were able to run faster. When they got to the shore Dani reached down to grab her clothes and then they were running back across the grass to the farm buildings.

They clambered through the hole in the wall by the pigsty and saw Paco by the barn door face turned to the sky looking for the approaching plane. Fernando ran over to the barn and pushed Paco inside.

"Not in there," gasped Elizabeth remembering she was almost naked. She grabbed Dani's hand and dragged him towards the farmhouse. Once inside they slammed the door shut and stood close together panting, listening for the sound of the enemy overhead. As their breathing began to quieten so they heard the wailing of the plane's engine as the pilot pitched to turn almost directly overhead. Dani felt sure he could hear his heart thumping out of control. He looked at Elizabeth's face just inches from his. Her skin was pale and perfect like fine china, drips of water running down from her wet hair. He could smell the soap she had been using to wash herself. Her eyes were a chestnut colour with occasional darker flecks and he felt like he was falling into them. Here was a man who had faced death on an almost daily basis for so long that he rarely felt frightened anymore, and yet here he was with this beautiful woman and he was scared to death. And then his eyes dropped to her mouth and there were suddenly butterflies in his stomach and his legs felt like they would buckle from under him. He wanted to kiss her more than he had ever wanted anything before in his life, but he hesitated because he wasn't sure what to do.

Elizabeth felt it too, like a spark shooting from his body to hers. Her whole being flushed red hot, when in reality it was freezing from the icy water of the lake. She thought he might be about to kiss her and she waited, trembling slightly, not sure how she would react if he did. But he made no move towards her, and they remained as close as two people can get without actually touching.

The plane had circled away without them realising, but now it was coming around again. Had the pilot seen them? Dani waited to hear the familiar rattle of machine guns, but there was nothing. As the aircraft flew directly over the farmhouse the noise of its single engine was deafening. Then it began to fade away into the distance.

At last Elizabeth moved, stepping back a pace. Dani realised that he was holding her clothes and offered them to her.

"I can't put these on top of my wet things," she whispered.

"I'll get you a blanket," said Dani, "then we'll put them in the sun to dry."

He left the farmhouse cautiously, ears pricked in case the plane made a return. In the barn he found Fernando and Paco sitting together on the tailgate of the lorry.

"That was a close one," laughed Fernando. "I think we gave our nurse a bit of a shock."

"Yes, we did," agreed Dani, "she's soaking so I'm going to take her a blanket and her things."

"Looks like you got a good soaking yourself," laughed Paco. Dani climbed up into the lorry, pushed past the other two and found a couple of blankets and Elizabeth's bag.

"You go and fill the water bottles will you Nando," asked Dani, "I need to dry off a bit."

"Sure," said the other man, jumping off the tailgate and heading towards the water once more.

Back at the farmhouse he found Elizabeth hiding behind her dry clothes. He handed her a blanket and her bag.

"You can get undressed in there," he told her indicating the tiny bedroom, "pass your wet things out to me and I'll find somewhere for them to dry. Dani turned his back to give her some privacy as the door had several panels missing and probably wouldn't have shut anyway. She moved into the other room and he heard the rustling of her movements and tried not to imagine what she might look like naked. After a while she called out to him and he went over and took her soaking undergarments. He had never touched a woman's under clothes before and he wasn't comfortable taking them from her. Seeing his awkwardness she squeezed his hand gently.

"Thank you Dani," she whispered.

"That's all right, listen you should stay in here and rest a while. That old mattress will probably be all right to sit on, but I should put the blanket on top of it."

"Yes, I will do, as soon as I finish drying my hair," and she used the blanket to towel her hair not dry but at least so that it was no longer dripping down onto her uniform.

Dani left her and found a secluded sunny spot along the stone wall to place her things to dry. He laid them out as quickly as he could trying not to get a good look at them. Then he hurried back to the barn, to change his underwear and put on his spare uniform which was in an even worse state than the one he had on. In a losing army new uniforms were impossible to come by, as was decent food, fuck, even bullets were hard to come by.

Fernando had returned with the water bottles, and they filled the lorry's radiator and stood and watched it slowly leak out through the hole where the metal had been impaled. Paco had removed it while Dani was changing, but it was obvious that the previous night the embedded piece of ironwork had sort of plugged its own hole and the water had only leaked out slowly. This had saved them from burning out the motor completely. Paco was going to try to plug the leak as best he could with an old rag jammed into the hole with a sliver of wood, but they would have to carry spare water with them and make sure to keep the radiator topped up. They emptied one of the fuel cans into the lorry's tank and Dani took it to the lake to wash it out and fill it with water. When he got there he found Elizabeth's shoes by the water's edge. He had been in too much of a hurry when he grabbed her uniform and they had been left behind. He would take them to her later after she had rested for a while. For now he wanted to write a bit in his diary about what had happened to them in the last twenty-four hours. Then he stretched out on a flat bit of grass to get some sleep. Sleep didn't come easily when you were being hunted like a fox.

*

The General stood outside his car puffing on a foul cigarette, sweating in the unaccustomed heat of this Mediterranean landscape. At last Alicante was in sight. Somehow they had made it from the airport at Albacete despite the poor state of the roads and the annoying numbers of refugees everywhere, not to mention enemy aircraft buzzing around. Down in the port below him he could see several anchored ships, one of which must be the one waiting to take him to South America. He wondered how far the lorry carrying his precious cargo had got. He had instructed his driver to make all possible haste and they had stuck to the main roads, but he knew the lorry would take a lot longer to get there, he just hoped that it would arrive in time. He couldn't delay his departure for very long, Alicante could be captured any day now, but he wanted to give the lorry every opportunity to arrive.

He finished his cigarette and stood for a few minutes looking out across the Mediterranean. It shimmered and snaked backwards and forwards and he knew it was his gateway to another life. He had been in Madrid throughout the whole war, he hadn't chosen the Republican side, he just happened to be in its territory at the wrong moment, but he had been determined not to die for a cause he couldn't have cared less about. And if the lorry arrived he would not have wasted his time in the Republic's service after all.

*

In the late afternoon, Captain Roberto Ruiz Roman arrived in the little village of Fuentidueña de Tajo. His driver stopped in the main square and Roberto saw a crowd of people grouped outside the town hall. He got out to stretch his legs and also to find out what was going on. There were a couple of Nationalist soldiers chatting to some local girls sitting on a bench but they seemed unconcerned about the fuss that was going on nearby. These two had obviously been left to keep order once the advanced troops had taken the town and were waiting for the main body of the army to catch up with them.

One of them saw the Captain approaching in his neat little uniform and nudged his friend with his elbow. The two soldiers straightened themselves up to full height in front of the local girls and gave their best matching salutes.

"What's going on here?" asked Roberto.

"Just some local dispute sir," said the slightly older of the two soldiers.

"What do you mean?"

"They're arguing about who should be executed or not, sir."

"So we leave it up to them do we?"

"We don't have orders to stop reprisals sir," put in the other soldier, "in fact we are normally encouraged to turn a blind eye. If people want to shoot the town Reds for us then we let them do it." He laughed. Roberto thought for a minute, he was, of course, all in favour of shooting Reds, but he just wanted to be sure that none of them had seen the phantom lorry that he was chasing.

"Okay you two, come with me. I need to ask a few questions before the killing starts." The two young men followed him not really happy to go looking for trouble where there hadn't been any. As they approached the mob Roberto drew his revolver and fired a shot in the air to announce his arrival. The squabbling stopped instantly and the crowd parted to let the soldiers through.

"Who's in charge here?" demanded the captain. Most of the men in the crowd turned to look at a middle-aged man with a fat belly despite three years of war. Roberto strode up to him and stood as close as he could in order to make him feel as uncomfortable as possible.

"Tell me what's going on," said Roberto.

"We're just deciding which of the Reds we're holding in the town hall are to be shot first."

"So they're all going to be shot?"

"Yes, I think so."

"And how many dangerous Reds have you got here?"

"About forty-five or fifty I would say."

"Really? Is that all? I would normally execute several hundred even in a small place like this. You haven't let any get away have you?"

"Some may have run away. Some were killed by the first troops who came through a few hours ago. The rest we'll get to tomorrow, this is just the first batch I would say."

"That's what I like to hear. And tell me, what gives you the authority here?"

"I used to be the Mayor here before all this Republic shit."

"That makes you the perfect man for the job then," agreed the captain nodding thoughtfully.

"Anyhow, señor Alcalde, I would just like to have a little chat with your Reds before they are rightfully shot, that's if you wouldn't mind that is."

"Not at all, be my guest," offered the ex-mayor, "follow me inside and I'll take you to them."

Roberto and his two borrowed soldiers followed the fat man into the ayuntamiento building and at the end of a long corridor they came to the Salón de Actos which was guarded by a couple of men holding rifles in such a way as to easily betray the fact that they weren't soldiers. The men stepped aside and the ex-mayor threw open the door. Inside, Roberto found more new soldiers with rifles they had recently acquired probably from the very men they now held captive.

"These are mostly members of the town militia and those who helped run the place for the Republic, communists all of them," said the ex-mayor.

"Who was the Mayor until today?" asked Roberto.

"We've already shot him. As soon as the town was liberated we stormed the town hall and found him in his office."

"That's good work," said Roberto appreciatively. "What about the leader of the militia?"

"He was killed in the fighting when the town was taken."

"That saves us the trouble then doesn't it? What about any Republican soldiers? Or did they all fight to the death?"

"Most of them ran away, we've got men out looking for them in the hills. There's only one here, a young boy really."

Roberto scanned the despondent men gathered there, no doubt all of them well aware that they were not going to live much longer. There at the back huddled against the wall was the young soldier the man had referred to.

"Fetch him here," Roberto ordered one of his soldiers. The man went over, grabbed the kid by the scruff of the neck and hauled him upright. He then pushed him over towards the Captain.

"Listen to me carefully you communist filth. I need some information. If you tell me something useful I might be able to spare your life, if you don't then you will be the first man to be shot here. Do you understand?" the boy soldier raised his stricken face with its wounded eyes and nodded at his enemy.

"I'm chasing a lorry that might have come through here in the last twenty-four hours or so. It would be a big heavy lorry, slow moving, obviously Republican." Roberto watched the man's face intently and was pleased to see a faint flicker of hope pass across his eyes. He obviously knew something.

NINE

"So," said Roberto, quietly, not wishing to startle the young man too much, "you saw a lorry coming through here."

"Yes sir. A big lorry, an ambulance." Roberto raised his eyebrows suspiciously, he wasn't looking for an ambulance, maybe this boy soldier wasn't going to be of any help after all.

"You should keep your mouth shut," shouted out an old man who was sitting on one of the long desks over by the right-hand wall.

Roberto turned to look at him, fuming. How dare he interrupt? The Captain turned and glared at the younger of his two soldiers.

"Shoot that man."

"Yes sir," responded the soldier although his voice didn't sound that full of confidence. He walked over to the man who had had the nerve to shout out and grabbed him by the arm. He pulled him down off the table and set to march him out of the room.

"No!" exploded Roberto, "here, now. I want it done right away. Right here in front of everyone."

The young soldier dropped the old man to the floor and stood looking down at him. He had never had to shoot anyone so close at hand before and with such a large audience too.

"Get on with it man," barked the Captain. He would have done it himself with pleasure, but he liked giving orders, especially orders to kill, especially to those who didn't want to do it. The young soldier released the safety on his rifle and raised it slowly with shaking hands. The old man seeing that he was about to be killed got unsteadily to his feet. The men who were nearest scampered away. The little old man raised himself up to his full height standing in front of the white wall and raised his clenched fist in defiant salute.

"Viva La República," he shouted. The young soldier fired. In the confined space of the meeting room the gun sounded like a canon going off. The bullet clipped the man in the right shoulder and sent him to the ground screaming in agony. Roberto acted quickly, pushing past the young soldier who still had his rifle pointing at the scarlet blood-spattered wall, where the old man had stood, and standing over the body writhing in agony on the floor he placed his pistol close to the man's head and fired. The body jerked down to the floor and was still, a big pool of black blood and brains slowly began to form on the earth-coloured floor tiles around it.

"Anyone else care to interrupt my work?" he asked the assembled captives waving his gun slowly around the group. There were no takers. There was complete silence. No one dared to breathe.

Captain Roberto walked back to the young soldier he had been talking to. He was fed up with wasting time. If the boy didn't know anything helpful then he would shoot him right there on the spot too.

"So, where were we? Oh yes, you said a lorry came through last night."

"An ambulance sir, a big one," stammered the boy soldier.

"Did I say I was looking for an ambulance?" growled Roberto directly into the soldier's face.

"No, but when I went to inspect their cargo they started shooting. My comrade was killed, I ran for my life."

"Cargo, an ambulance carrying a cargo you say?"

"Yes sir," managed the boy shaking like a leaf, trying to control his bladder and his chattering teeth at the same time. Perhaps it could be true thought Roberto. No one had told his pilots to look for an ambulance. What a clever thing to do, use an ambulance. The more he thought about it, the more convinced he became that this was indeed the lorry he was looking for.

"What happened to the lorry?" asked Roberto more quietly now.

"It got through our road block and drove through the town. The militia chased it I think, sir."

Roberto turned to look at the other captured men in the room.

"Who here was in the militia and wants to have the chance to save his life?" he offered. No one moved. "Okay, I'll count to ten and then we'll start shooting people. One, two."

"He was in the militia," said someone pointing at the dead old man on the floor. Roberto went straight over to the man who had spoken and held his pistol to his temple.

"Three, four, five, six, seven," Roberto continued to count.

"The militia chased the lorry to the bridge," gushed the man.

"And what happened?"

The man seemed to hesitate.

"Eight, nine."

"They used dynamite to blow the bridge."

"They blew the bridge?"

"Well, not entirely blew the bridge, just sort of damaged it a bit."

"Your troops did a quick repair when they discovered it," said the ex-mayor helpfully from nearby.

"And we can drive across it?" asked the Captain.

"I think so, they took all their armoured vehicles across earlier."

"Good. I've wasted enough time in this godforsaken putrid shithole already."

"What should I do with these men?" asked the fat ex-mayor.

"You were going to shoot them weren't you?"

"Yes we were."

"So carry on. This one goes first," he said indicating the man who had told him about the bridge, "line them up in the square for all to see and shoot the lot of them. Don't delay. These two soldiers will be in the firing squad, they need the practice. Anyone who says Viva la República, shoot their family too."

"What about the boy?"

Roberto realised that he still had his pistol in his hand. He went over to the captured Red soldier and shot him in the head.

"Problem solved," he stated as the soldier crumpled at his feet without even a murmur.

Roberto marched purposefully back across the square the waiting crowd of onlookers parting to let him through. Those who had relatives inside the town hall hoped that the mysterious Rebel captain had decided that the captured men shouldn't be shot, the others hoped that they would be. The Captain climbed into his staff car and told his driver to get going again. They headed through the narrow streets of the village until they came to the bridge across the Tajo. It was a long iron bridge and as they crossed, the scars of an explosion were clearly visible at about the half way point. At the next village Roberto would try to find a field telephone to call the air force base and let them know that the lorry they were looking for was an ambulance. For now he simply wanted to put as much distance as possible between himself and the River Tajo. They started to climb up the far bank. Roberto realised that a heavy lorry would have found this steep valley road hard going and he was happy that he must surely be catching up with them. He knew now exactly what he was looking for and he was hot on their trail.

*

As dusk approached, Dani went to the farmhouse to wake the sleeping nurse. He found her sitting on the blanket on the floor.

"We're nearly ready to get going again," he told her. "We should be able to reach Albacete by dawn. Who knows we might even get a decent bed at the barracks there if we're lucky."

"I'll settle for a decent breakfast," said Elizabeth.

"Are you hungry again?" asked Dani.

"I've been hungry since we left Madrid."

"I've been hungry since my mother last made me a *puchero*," he responded.

"What's a *puchero*?"

"It's a southern dish, turkey thighs, an old ham bone, some beef maybe, potatoes, turnips, carrots and chickpeas in a kind of stew. My father hated it, but I loved it."

"Stop it! My stomach's starting to ache," she complained. Dani laughed and fished into his jacket pocket and pulled out some pine nuts.

"Here, take these. We've got plenty more."

"Where did you get these?"

"Fernando and Paco got them last night when they went into the pine forest. Nando gave me a handful just now. A soldier never misses a chance to grab anything edible when he can."

"I need to think more like a soldier," said the nurse. Dani laughed. "If you want some more just ask the others. They're not much but they'll stop your stomach complaining all night. We'll see what we can scrounge when we get to Albacete."

"Have you been to Albacete before?" she wanted to know.

"Yes, I was there for about a month a year or so ago, Nando and I went there to help train some of the new Internationals, Albacete was the training base for newly-arrived foreigners."

"Has Fernando been everywhere with you?"

"Yes, we've always been together since we were kids. When we were little we used to look for crabs and limpets in the rock pools and take them home for our mothers to put into the fish head soup."

"Oh no, not food again," she groaned and she popped a pine nut into her mouth. She would have eaten the whole handful at once, but Dani had told her to make them last all night and so that's what she would try to do. It was going to be another long and fretful night she could feel it.

She followed Dani out of the house carrying her bag with her few personal possessions. Dani took her to where her underwear had been left to dry and she quickly slipped it inside her bag. She felt embarrassed that he had had to handle her most intimate garments and she blushed slightly. Dani collected his spare uniform from nearby and they went over to the barn where the other two were waiting, faces looking up to the heavens, searching for nightfall. They were all impatient to get on their way, but if they left too early and were caught out in the open by an enemy plane then they would be sitting ducks. And so they waited. Paco had spoken about the route they would take, through the Sierras, leaving the Valencia Highroad and cutting through the hills southwards to join the road to Albacete at La Roda, less than forty kilometres from Albacete. Those last few kilometres were the only ones that they would travel on the main road and therefore they would be the most dangerous. Dani hoped they would be able to get there well before daybreak.

There was always the possibility that the Nationalists had advanced so far during the day that they were now behind enemy lines. Perhaps Albacete had already been taken. There was no way of knowing. There was nothing to do except to press on and hope for the best. Dani had already decided that he would rather die fighting than let himself be captured, and he was determined that their valuable cargo, whatever it was, wouldn't be captured either. The thought that the cargo they were transporting might be a way of guaranteeing their safety crossed his mind like a dark shadow, but Dani dismissed this possibility and hated the fact that it had even occurred to him, even in the darkest recesses of his mind.

*

Captain Roberto Ruiz Roman reached Tarancón and found that he could get no further. This was where the Nationalist advanced units were stopping for the night. He cursed at the local commander but the man was adamant that they would go nowhere until first light. His men had been clearing their way through barricaded villages all day and were in need of rest. Everyone had their nerves on edge. These were the last hours of the war and no one wanted to take any unnecessary risks and cop a bullet when they were so close to the end of hostilities. He'd lost twenty men during the course of the day. Roberto's driver was exhausted too, they had spent the whole day on the move and he was in need of some sleep.

The commander found Roberto a room at a rundown inn and the lady who ran it had some watery chicken soup on the stove, the smell of which reminded the Captain that he hadn't eaten all day. It made you hungry this work that he did, killing people. It made you thirsty too. He told the woman to take a bowl of soup out to his driver who would sleep in the car during the night to make sure that nothing happened to it. These were terrible times and there could still be people here in this town desperate to escape, and a staff car with petrol might prove an irresistible target. When the woman returned she found Roberto seated at a wooden table in the dining room waiting for his meal. She hadn't offered him food but he didn't look like the sort of person you really wanted to cross. She ladled out a generous bowl of the soup, which was mostly water since the chicken bones it contained had been boiled up every evening for a week. She had used it to feed up her sons before they fled into the high sierras to avoid the approaching fascists. She placed the bowl on the table in front of the captain and handed him a spoon. She turned to walk away but he grabbed her savagely by the wrist.

"Get me some wine woman," he hissed.

"Are you out of your mind? Where in hell would I have wine after all these months of war? Don't you think if there was wine here I'd have drunk it myself?"

"I know you people produce wine in this area, I saw the vineyards all along the Tajo valley. If there's no wine in this house then you'd better send out for some."

"Do you really think there's likely to be a drop of wine left in town with hundreds of your soldiers milling around?"

"Get me some wine or I'll have your children shot."

"My sons are long dead and my daughter is a whore in Albacete. If you go there give her my regards before you shoot her."

"Go and tell my driver to get me some wine," he told her.

"Tell him yourself," said the woman and she went back to the kitchen to get a bowl of soup. Roberto watched her. He liked the way she was unafraid of him, but he would have to sleep with the door locked and one eye open with this one around. He left the table and went out to the car where his driver had just finished his soup.

"I want you to get me some wine, and some brandy too if there is any in this place."

"What about the car?"

"You'd better hurry up. If anything happens to the car while you're gone I'll shoot you myself." The Captain produced a folded one peseta note from his jacket pocket and passed it to the driver. A Nationalist note would be worth more than gold in this so recently Republican area where their own pesetas were now worthless. Then he went back inside. The night air was starting to get cold already and he fancied another bowl of soup.

Just as he was finishing his second helping of the woman's watery soup his driver came in bringing a wave of cold with him. He placed a goatskin of wine on the table and produced a bottle of Fundador brandy from inside his jacket the new Nationalist one peseta note had done the trick. The driver left to sleep in the cold car.

"You see woman, there is wine in this place and even brandy you just have to know where to look for it. Bring me a glass I don't want to drink from a smelly old goatskin."

The woman went to a cupboard under the sink and came over with two small glasses. She picked up the goat skin and pulled open the stopper with her teeth and then poured the dark wine. They sat and drank in silence. When the woman had finished her glass she got up to leave him alone to get drunk. He caught her wrist once more.

"I wouldn't mind some company tonight it gets lonely always being on the move you know."

"Go find my daughter in Albacete," the woman told him and shook herself free from his grasp. She had already decided that this man was here to hunt down her sons and their friends. She had also decided that when he was drunk she would slit his fascist throat.

TEN

At last it seemed dark enough for them to get under way. The sun had finally vanished behind the distant mountain peaks. Paco fired up the engine which spluttered and came to life, much to everyone's relief. They left the farmhouse behind them and skirted around the shore of the lake to pick up the little road through the Sierras and south to link up eventually with the Madrid-Albacete-Alicante Highroad. They hadn't been able to take this route out of Madrid, as part of the road had been in Nationalist hands since the Battle of Jarama in early 1937 when the Rebels had tried to encircle the Republican capital.

After three kilometres the bumpy track by the lake joined the road and the going got a little easier although it was very much a minor road. They were now driving through the Sierra del Pintado, slipping between the highest peaks, the lorry struggling with its load. Dani was glad that it wasn't raining like the previous night.

They drove for a long time without seeing a soul, with just the mountain peaks for company like distant cousins. It was quiet in the cab and it was quiet in the back. Fernando was stretched out on the floor with Elizabeth sitting behind him wrapped in blankets. The temperature had dropped steadily since they had left and there was no heating in the back of the lorry. Surely it would be warmer when they reached the coast thought Elizabeth. She had known the extreme cold of that last winter of war in besieged Madrid when there had been nothing left to burn. She had preferred to work at night because at least in the packed hospital wards there was the heat generated by all those wounded bodies together. In her little bed back at the nurses' digs she just spent the nights listening to her teeth chattering uncontrollably. She could have taken an extra blanket from the hospital like some of the other nurses, but her conscience wouldn't let her. The wounded soldiers had little to make them comfortable as it was. Many of them sobbed quietly throughout the long hours of darkness. Some cried out in their sleep tormented by terrible nightmares of the events they had witnessed. The older ones would call out for their wives and the younger ones for their mothers or for a girl from home who had become an imagined sweetheart to help see them through the war.

66

Elizabeth wondered if she would ever forget what she had lived through in Madrid. When she was back in the family house would she still dream of the faces of dead men? Would the smell of bleach always remind her of blood and make her want to vomit? Would she always feel sad in her heart every time someone mentioned Spain?

*

Captain Roberto Ruiz Roman could drink no more. He had drunk the putrid-smelling red wine until he wanted to throw up and then he had opened the bottle of brandy. It was better than a lot of *coñac* he had had to bear during this war, but he still preferred whisky. The brandy took away the taste of the wine and mulled his thoughts. He was still annoyed with the woman for rejecting him. After all, she was definitely nothing special to look at. When would she get another offer from someone like him? Maybe she still believed that her husband would come back from whatever prisoner of war camp he had ended up in. Roberto would tell her in the morning that he had probably been shot within hours of being captured, that was the Nationalist way.

He somehow managed to stand up by pushing down with both hands on the table. He stood there swaying for a bit waiting for the room to stop spinning. He liked being like this, he knew he would be able to sleep peacefully without being tormented by nightmares. He grabbed the bottle of brandy from the table and with one hand against the wall he stumbled out of the kitchen to the bottom of the stairs. He waited for a while to get his sights set on where he had to go, and then he began to climb up a step at a time. It was slow going. About half way up, the bottle of Fundador slipped from his hand and bumped down the wooden stairs to smash on the tiled floor at the bottom. He cursed his bad luck but then realised that he was able to use two hands to support his weight and so he was able to get to the top of the stairs a lot more quickly. His room was the first one on the left-hand side and he could hear loud snores from behind the other doors further along the corridor. He wondered where the woman slept, but decided it was too complicated, burst through his own door, staggered three steps towards the middle of the room and crashed down on the bed. Within seconds he had started to snore.

*

After what seemed like forever, the lorry approached a small mountain village. Paco slowed slightly as he always did in case they came upon a road block or something. Just at the entrance to the village was the cemetery and as they got near they saw a small lorry blocking the road. There were dark shapes scurrying around like ants which turned into men as they drew closer. When they became aware of the approaching ambulance the men crowded together into the road to find out who had arrived in the dead of night at their little forgotten village.

"What's going on?" asked Paco.

"I don't know," replied Dani, his voice not more than a whisper. Paco brought the lorry to a halt alongside the group of men who were in the road. Dani wound down his window to talk to them.

"What's going on here?" he demanded trying to keep an air of authority in his voice.

"We're just shooting some Reds," said a middle-aged man, "thought we'd save you lot the trouble." Dani realised that he had assumed that they were the first of the Rebel forces to arrive rather than the last of the Popular Army. It was understandable given the situation, given that is was dark and given that the war had probably passed this little mountain village by. Then why, wondered Dani were they suddenly about to start shooting people? The Captain opened the door and got out.

"Keep your gun handy Paco and keep the engine running in case anything happens." Paco moved for his rifle which was tucked down behind his seat. He shut the door and shouted to Fernando to come with his weapon. Fernando had been on alert as soon as they had stopped, he handed a pistol to Elizabeth in case she needed it, and was quickly at the Captain's side. They walked over towards the dirty-white wall of the village cemetery where they saw a couple of dead bodies on the ground and six men standing heads bowed waiting to join them.

"What's their crime?" Dani asked the leader of the group who seemed to be shadowing him.

"They're Reds," replied the man.

"So you said, but what crime did they commit against this village?"

"They ran the farming cooperative, they're communists."

"And did they kill anyone?"

"He wants us shot because the farming cooperative took his father's land," called out one of the men waiting to be executed.

"Is that true?" Dani wanted to know.

"That land is mine. It's my birthright," replied the leader of the execution party defiantly.

"And you'll get it back now that the war is over, so why shoot these men?"

"Because they're the enemy."

"They're not my enemy," said Dani quietly. The man suddenly realised the mistake he had made of assuming that these soldiers were Rebels. Dani placed his gun at the man's temple.

"On my god!" gasped the man.

"You men there, go back to the village, take what you need and disappear into the mountains. Maybe you should take your families too, but hurry."

"Thank you comrade," said the man who had spoken out before, tears of relief starting to tumble from his eyes. He came over and hugged Dani.

"Viva la República," shouted another.

"Go quickly," Dani told them. "Take that lorry, get your families and flee."

The men didn't need to be told twice and they quickly started to move towards the vehicle which had brought them out to the cemetery in the first place. Dani was just beginning to think that he had pulled it off, when one of the men who had been in the firing squad realised that they outnumbered these newcomers. He raised his rifle and shot one of the escaping men in the back. Suddenly all hell broke loose. The man next to Dani tried to twist away from him and the Captain instantly shot him in the head. Fernando meanwhile had his rifle at his shoulder and fired at the man who had started it all. Dani dropped to his knees so as to present less of a target and fired at another of the men with a gun. The remaining five prisoners ran for the road as fast as they could. One of them fell to the ground as a shot rang out. At that moment Paco arrived on the scene and fired a couple of shots and then it was all over just as suddenly as it had begun. There was only one person left with a rifle, a young lad who had been too scared to actually fire his weapon during the fight, and seeing himself the only one left armed, he dropped the rifle to the floor and flung his arms up in the air in surrender.

"Don't shoot me," he begged turning a ghostlike face towards Dani. Paco approached and levelled his weapon at the boy who dropped to his knees still holding his hands up.

"That's enough Paco," shouted the Captain. "You and Fernando round up the others from the road and bring them over here." Paco seemed to hesitate for a moment, and then reluctantly turned and walked with Fernando towards the road. Someone decided to make a run for it back towards the village and Paco quickly raised his rifle and shot the man in the back. The man's legs crumpled beneath him and he tumbled into a ditch at the roadside. The remaining men raised their hands in surrender and allowed themselves to be shepherded over towards the cemetery wall where the firing squad had been. Those who had escaped execution climbed into the little lorry that had brought them from the village and set off back towards their homes. No doubt they wouldn't last long as fugitives up in the mountains, but at least they had the chance to escape for now.

"Are you going to shoot us?" one of the captured men wanted to know.

"Do I need to?" asked Dani.

"No, we won't cause you any trouble," replied the man. The others quickly agreed with him nodding earnestly.

"We ought to shoot them Comrade Captain," suggested Paco.

"No, please, Dani," shouted Elizabeth who had climbed down from the lorry gun in hand to see who had won the fight. She was relieved to see that her men were unscathed, but she didn't want to witness a murder taking place.

"The war's over Paco," Dani told him. "Let's leave here and get on our way. These men have families and besides, what's Spain going to do in the future if we all shoot each other?"

Paco gave an exaggerated shrug of his shoulders.

"What do I care about a fascist Spain?" he said.

"Spain won't stay fascist forever," replied Dani. "There's already talk of a European war. Maybe the Fascists will be defeated and the Republic will rise again."

"I doubt it," mumbled Paco.

70

"Come on, let's get back on the road, we've still got a long way to go tonight. If we can reach Albacete we should be safe for a while," said Dani. They walked away leaving a small group of very relieved men behind them and of course several dead bodies, some had been Communists some had been Rebels, all of them were equally dead. They would all be buried together in the same cemetery, side by side, just as previous generations had been before the war.

*

The woman had been lying still in her bed since hearing the bottle fall down the stairs and smash at the bottom. She had half expected the brutal Captain to try to force his way into her room. The door was bolted but she wasn't convinced that that would be enough to stop him. She had her husband's hunting knife hidden under her pillow in case her door was broken down. When nothing happened she just lay still for as long as she could bear, her heart pounding, listening to the giant snores of the men who had been sent to stay with her. When she was convinced that the Captain must be asleep she got out of bed and dressed quickly. As soon as he was dead she would flee to the hills to be with her sons.

Quietly, she pulled back the bolt on her door. It squeaked suddenly and she froze, heart in mouth. After a few minutes she tried again and this time there wasn't a sound. Before opening the door she reached under her pillow and got the knife and then slipped out of her room. She could just make out at the end of the corridor that the Captain's door was wide open, there was moonlight too, meaning he hadn't bothered to close the shutters before going to bed. Perhaps he was still awake. The thought terrified her. Then there came a loud snort and the sound of the old metal bedstead groaning as the man changed position. In fact it was Roberto pulling himself into the middle of the bed.

The woman waited again. Paralysed by fear and yet determined to do something she was convinced would help her sons. A thunderous new bout of snoring cannoned out of the room and the woman crept towards the doorway on tiptoes. When she got to the entrance to the Captain's room she peeked round and saw him now lying in the middle of the bed, curled in a ball like a large sleeping child. He was still fully dressed he hadn't even taken off his boots. He was lying on top of the blankets, despite the cold.

The woman moved towards the bed and raised the knife. She made the mistake of looking at his face which in sleep didn't seem quite as brutal as earlier on, and she hesitated just a second before stabbing him. It must have been some sort of soldier's instinct that made Roberto aware of the danger he was in, perhaps soldiers in a war can never really fall into a deep enough sleep to be able to dull out what is going on around them, whatever it was Roberto opened his eyes just at the second when the woman had her moment of hesitation. He was suddenly fully awake and reached up and grabbed her arm with both hands. The woman pushed against him with all her strength, but it was no use, she was no match for this toughened soldier. Slowly Roberto came up to a sitting position and from there he was able to place one foot onto the floor. As soon as he had managed that it was easy for him to flip the woman and smash her down onto the bed. With the wind knocked out of her she loosened her grip on the knife and Roberto snatched it from her. He held it to her throat.

In the patchy moonlight the veins on her neck stood out clearly and in a professional way Roberto admired their beauty. As he sliced the knife across her throat he felt supremely powerful as the first signs of blood began to appear blurring the edges of the neat cut he had made. He looked into the woman's startled eyes. It had all happened so quickly that she couldn't believe what had taken place. The last thing she was aware of was the oddly smiling face of her killer wicked in the half light.

ELEVEN

Dani was relieved to be making progress having been held up so early on. They left the little mountain village behind to sort out its problems without them. Once more alone on the road and shrouded by darkness it came to him how close he had been to death once more. It was strange, the first time he had been in a gunfight he had been too scared to fire and everything that had gone on around him had happened in slow motion and it was almost as if he wasn't actually there. When it was all over he found himself shaking uncontrollably his rifle still down at his side unused. But now, in the face of danger he was calm and controlled. That was the big difference an experienced soldier made in battle. And Dani had known his fair share of battles in this war.

After a while, they came across a windmill looming up out of the darkness, its giant arms still and in disrepair, and Dani was reminded that they were in Don Quijote country. It occurred to him that they ought to stop and check the radiator, fill it up with water maybe and also put some more petrol into the tank. He told Paco to pull over by the entrance to the windmill. It was a round stone building topped by a pointed roof which had seen better days and of course the four sail arms hanging limp and unused. When they stopped Dani went to the rear to tell Fernando to take the water to Paco who was already peering at the radiator with his American torch.

"Elizabeth, you should come and see this windmill," Dani suggested. The English nurse got up from the floor of the truck and struggled over to the back of the lorry, her legs had gone to sleep having been curled up beneath her for so long. As she tried to get down to the ground her right leg gave way and she slipped. Fortunately, Dani reacted quickly and caught her in his arms. He was taken by surprise and just stood still with her face inches from his own, her eyes bright and alive in the moonlight. They separated quickly when they heard Fernando returning to get a can of petrol. Elizabeth walked over towards the windmill to get a better look.

"This is the last can," said Fernando climbing down from the back of the lorry.

"We should be able to get to Albacete, shouldn't we?" asked Dani.

"I think so."

"I wonder if we can get some more petrol there?"

"It might be difficult. Anyone with a motor vehicle will be looking for petrol."

"We've got the General's orders, but they might not mean much at this stage. Everyone's going to be looking out for themselves by now."

"How far behind us do you think the Rebels are Dani?"

"I don't know Nando, but we've got to assume that they're right behind us. Come on *amigo*, let's get going again." He walked over to find Elizabeth who was at the back of the windmill.

"It's really beautiful, isn't it?" she asked.

"Yes, it is. Spain's a beautiful country you just haven't seen it at its best that's all."

"No, I guess not. Everyone told me that Madrid was such a fine city, but when I got there it was so shattered."

"It will be a fine city again one day. Maybe you can return and see it in better times."

"Maybe," she said although she sounded doubtful. At this moment all she wanted to do was put as much distance as possible between herself and the Spanish capital. It was all she could do from bursting into tears at her situation. This trip had made her aware that she was in very real danger, and she was beginning to realise just how stupid she had been to come to a foreign country in the middle of a war. She could have got out when the other non-Spanish nurses left, that would have been the sensible thing to do, but no, she had to remain. How could she have been so naive? And now all she could do was to feel sorry for herself and promise herself that if she did manage to escape death in this foreign land that she would never be so stupid again. A calm and monotonous life in Bournemouth in the bosom of her family suddenly seemed so appealing.

Dani saw her wipe a tear from the corner of her eye and automatically stepped towards her in a gesture of comfort. Before either of them realised what was happening she was in his arms once more. She closed her eyes tight shut and concentrated on the feel of his strong arms around her and somehow managed to keep back the urge to cry. Their situation was hopeless, but if Dani still desperately believed that they could succeed then she would try to match his determination. She took a deep

74

breath and pulled back slightly from Dani's embrace. He held her at arm's length for a moment and then he took her by the hand and led her back towards the lorry. As they got near he let go of her hand before the others saw them. They went their separate ways once more.

After a while they approached a crossroads where their little mountain track joined the road that formally linked the Valencia Highroad to the Alicante Highroad. They could see that there was a roadblock, but there didn't appear to be anyone around. Paco slowed the lorry down to a crawl and then stopped altogether in front of a makeshift barrier of old tables and sideboards. They waited on tenterhooks for a couple of minutes, both with their guns at the ready. They were expecting a shot to ring out or at least a challenge of some sort but there was nothing, just the throb of the motor in front of them.

Dani peered out of the cab into the darkness. They were down in a cut which had been made to bring their track down to the level of the road it had to cross, and anyone could have been hiding above and out of view. If he left the safety of the cab he might well be greeted by a hail of bullets from soldiers who assumed that the enemy they had been waiting for had arrived. He swallowed hard and opened the door just an inch or two, ready to slam it shut again if a shot rang out. After a pause to allow his heart beat to calm a little Dani opened the door a bit more. Still nothing happened and now he opened it sufficiently to be able to climb out.

"If I get shot just drive straight through the barrier and keep going," he told Paco who was scanning the high ground rifle at the ready.

Dani jumped down from the cab his feet crunching into the dirt. He kept low, presenting as small a target as possible and looked left and right for any signs of danger. Nothing moved. He eased his way to the back of the lorry and called out to Fernando to bring his rifle. When his friend was there to offer some sort of covering fire, he separated himself from the lorry and started up the slope to check out the high ground. He felt more exposed than ever in his life, crouching low, waiting for the impact of a bullet, his ears straining ahead into the darkness where his eyes couldn't reach. At last at the top of the rise he was able to see that there was no one over on this side. He lay down flat and pointed his revolver back across the top of the ambulance towards the other side of the road. He called out to Fernando that he should go check it out and watched as his friend moved away from the protection of the lorry. Once more he expected to hear a shot ring out. Fernando made his way slowly up the other slope, keeping low just as Dani had done. Once at the top he waved his arms to let the others know that it was clear. Dani rushed back down, slipping on loose stones, and called to Fernando to return. Then they set about dismantling the barricade. They worked as quickly as they could since they were still sitting ducks if anyone came along and decided to shoot at them. They worked up a good sweat despite the chill mountain air, throwing aside the odd pieces of bent and broken furniture that someone had gone to the trouble to build but then mysteriously leave unmanned.

*

The General watched the girl undress in the moonlight coming in through his hotel window. This was the best room he had been able to find in Alicante although it was nothing special and this girl was supposedly the best girl his adjutant had been able to find and she was definitely nothing special. She was so thin that the General's bulk on top of her might break her clearly-visible ribs. When she had finished unbuttoning the front of her dress he was not surprised to see that her breasts were tiny. He had been hoping for something with a bit more flesh on it, something to take his mind off the damned lorry that was keeping him waiting, but this girl wasn't about to do that. He played with the fat cigar between his lips as he lay back on the bed watching her disinterested striptease. Maybe he might burn her with it and make her scream, that might get his juices flowing. He gave a load sigh and decided that he would rather spend the night alone.

The girl dropped her dress to the tiled floor and stood, arms folded across her chest, looking at the fat man on the bed in full uniform. She had taken a large handful of worthless Republican notes for this, but maybe she hadn't asked enough. When the city fell to the Fascists she would start to make some decent Burgos money she promised herself. She knew that the few whores who had chosen to remain in this beleaguered port would make a killing when the victorious Nationalist soldiers began to celebrate the end of the war. This was her last Republican job she decided. When she got away from this fat and repulsive General then she would find an abandoned warehouse to hide away in until the city was liberated. And she would hail the Fascists as saviours as loud as anyone, and she would work day and night while the going was easy. And then she would take her money back to the *pueblo* where she had grown up and marry the first decent farmer she could find.

"You can go," growled the General with a dismissive wave of his pudgy hand.

"What Comrade General?" she asked not sure that she had understood him.

"Get the fuck out of here," he shouted finally removing the cigar from his mouth. The girl bent down, grabbed her dress and ran to the door, she didn't need telling twice. She was out of the room before he remembered that she had been paid already. Still, what did it matter? The Republican peseta was dead and the notes weren't worth a thing now.

When she was gone, the General raised himself up off the bed and went over to the window. There was a good view of the harbour and there in front of him he could make out the ship that was waiting to take him into exile. She was a single-funnelled steamer, black-hulled in the darkness upon the shattered-glass water. He knew the Captain was impatient to leave. Every tide they missed made the man more nervous. There were thousands of refugees already in Alicante and thousands more on the roads heading that way, all hoping that there would be a ship waiting to take them to safety. For most people there would be no chance of a place on a ship, the lucky few were those like the General who had promised a large sum of money to a ship's captain.

He stayed for a while at the window looking at his ship and wondering what his new life would be like in Mexico. He would be a rich man, an unbelievably rich man, but only if that damned lorry arrived in time. He clutched at his fat stomach where his ulcer had suddenly begun to rage. It was a good job that the girl had gone since he might have shot her just to relieve his intense feeling of frustration. If the lorry didn't arrive in the morning he really would have to shoot someone.

*

When Dani and Fernando had cleared a large enough hole, Paco eased the lorry through the barricade and across the main road. They set off once again. As the road levelled out, away to their right Dani could make out a tiny village dominated by a ruined castle overlooking a cluster of houses. They had just started to pick up speed to get them away from the roadblock when there was an almighty bang as the front right tyre burst. The lorry lurched violently across the road. Paco fought with the wheel and slammed on the brakes, but the lorry was out of control and it veered off the track and down a small slope before finally coming to a thumping halt in a drainage ditch at the bottom.

TWELVE

Dani was the first one out of the lorry and went to the back to check on the others. They had been thrown around a bit but were not injured. It was a good job that their heavy load was well strapped down otherwise there would have been heavy crates flying all over the place and the two passengers in the rear could well have been crushed. Paco remained in the cab with the engine running, first trying to back out up the slope and then trying to drive forward out of the ditch. But the lorry wouldn't budge the drive wheels were off the ground and spinning uselessly in the air. All four together tried to push the lorry backwards but they couldn't get it to move an inch. Realizing that they were not going to have any success Dani went back up to the road to think. Paco stayed down in the ditch with his flashlight checking the front of the ambulance for further damage, but the other two went after the Captain. They found him staring at the nearby village.

"What can we do?" asked Feranando.

"The only thing we can do is to go into the village and ask for help," said Dani.

"Isn't that going to be dangerous?" asked the nurse.

"Yes, of course, but what choice do we have? If we stay here until dawn and the Rebels find us we're done for."

"Let's get cracking then," decided Fernando.

"You come with us Elizabeth, with you along we might be able to make them believe that we're an ambulance crew urgently needed in Albacete."

Dani went to tell Paco of their plan and also to get the driver's rifle. He would be no use in a fight with just a revolver. Paco handed him his gun and a handful of spare bullets which Dani slipped into his jacket pocket.

"If we're not back by dawn use the dynamite to blow up the lorry and then run for the hills," Dani instructed him. Paco grunted in response and went back to peering at the engine.

The two soldiers and the nurse set off walking along the road towards the village. As they passed the roadblock they saw that the track on either side was littered with debris and they must have driven over a piece of metal from an ancient bedstead or over a piece of wood with a nail sticking out. They were lucky that they had only punctured one tyre. The lorry would have one spare but no more.

The village wasn't far away and yet the only sounds were the noise of their feet crunching in the gravel of the road and the insane laughter of a donkey from somewhere up ahead. The two men readied their rifles as they approached the first of the small white houses. Everywhere was ghostly quiet almost as if all the people had decided to leave rather than to face the Rebel army. Maybe that was why their barricade had been unmanned.

Dani knocked loudly on an old wooden door. There wasn't a sound from the house within. Fernando knocked on another further along the road, again there was no reply. And so they walked through the main street, knocking on doors and getting no response. Eventually they reached the church. Like so many churches it had been burnt out in the first weeks of the Republic when the ordinary people had turned against the Catholic Church which had oppressed them for so long. And yet, its huge gothic stone walls remained to dominate the village as they had done for centuries. The roof might have gone and the altar might have been smashed to pieces, but the symbol remained dominating the heart of the place.

They came to a halt beside one of the massive buttress walls of the church and looked around them. Suddenly, a shot rang out from nowhere and a bullet thudded into the stone wall above them. Instinctively the three of them ducked and ran back along the side of the church. Another shot rang out and this time Dani realized that they were being fired on from higher ground and that could only mean that someone was in the ruined castle which stood up on top of the hill. In a way it was a relief that this wasn't just a ghost town, but now they had to try to persuade the people that they weren't the enemy. Of course it was possible that all those who might be identified with the Republic had fled leaving behind a few Rebel sympathisers to welcome the victors, in which case they were never going to get any help at all.

They moved carefully away from the castle's line of fire and kept behind the houses moving slowly up the hill. When they came to the last house and could go no further without coming out into the open, Dani decided that they were within shouting distance.

"Comrades," he yelled out. He was greeted by the crack of a rifle and a bullet clipped the corner of the wall behind which they were hiding. "Stop shooting. We are Republicans." There was a silence. "We are soldiers of the Popular Army, we've come from Madrid," Dani continued to call out.

"How do we know you're not Fascists?"

"Let me come out, unarmed, I can show you my orders. We're a medical crew and we need to get to Albacete urgently. Our ambulance crashed off the road and we need help to get it out of a ditch."

"Okay, come out slowly, hands in the air. We won't shoot."

Dani took a deep breath, gave the other two a little false smile to try to show them some confidence he didn't possess, and propping his rifle up against the wall of the house he stepped out with his hands raised. His neck was pressed as far down into his jacket as it would go and his back was hunched so that he felt as small as possible. His whole body was tensed up in the hope that a bullet might just bounce off him. He raised his eyes up towards the castle and at a gap in the ruined battlements he could make out the shape of man and a small boy walking through the rubble towards him. The man was pointing an ancient rifle in Dani's direction with one hand and holding the boy's hand with the other.

"Where's everyone else?" asked Dani.

"They've all gone to Belmonte to make a last stand there," the man explained. "We couldn't go because my wife is in labour. I managed to carry her up here to the castle, but she's about to give birth. I don't know what to do."

"It's okay, there's a nurse with us," Dani informed him. He called out to Elizabeth and Fernando to come out from where they were hiding.

"This man's wife is having a baby up there in the castle," Dani told the nurse, "go and see what you can do."

"Take the nurse to your mother *hijo*," the man instructed his son. The boy took Elizabeth's hand and led her up towards the gap in the castle wall.

"We really needed a large group of people to help push our ambulance out of the ditch," Dani told the man rubbing his hand through his hair in frustration.

"I've got my mules," the man informed him.

"What?" asked Dani.

"My mules. I've got eight mules, I run the mule train from here to Belmonte every day. You know, buying and selling things for people."

"Where are they?"

"Here in the castle. We brought everything we own up here with us. We didn't want to leave anything for the fascists."

"But you didn't really think that you could hold off the whole Rebel army just you and your son and eight mules, did you?"

"No. We planned to get away as soon as we could or to lay low here in the castle. It was my son who fired at you, he was on watch while I was trying to help my wife and he got a bit excited."

"Can we borrow your animals?"

"Sure. Let's get them unloaded and we'll take a look at your ambulance."

"Don't you want to stay with your wife?"

"What can I do? Besides, when the boy was born I fainted at the first sight of blood," laughed the man.

Fernando and Dani helped the man and his son unload their possessions from the mules whilst all the while from over in the shadows of the far wall came the whimpering cries of the woman in labour and the reassuring murmur of Elizabeth's quiet instructions. Dani hadn't asked the nurse if she had delivered a baby before or not, maybe he had been afraid of the answer.

Back along the road they found Paco sitting having a smoke. He jumped to his feet when he heard the braying of the approaching mules and couldn't believe his eyes when he saw Dani and Fernando coming along with them.

"Dios Mío!" exclaimed the driver. "Where did you find all those beasts?"

"Don't ask," laughed Dani.

They soon had the eight mules roped up together and the rope attached to the back axel of the lorry. Dani and Fernando went down into the ditch to help push and Paco started the engine. When the mule driver gave his command Paco put the lorry into reverse and Dani and Fernando pushed for all they were worth. At first it seemed as though nothing would happen, but then Dani realized that the ambulance was just starting to move, slowly an inch or two at a time until it rocked over slightly and its drive wheels were able to get a grip. Feeling his wheels bite in the dirt Paco accelerated and the lorry began to claw its way up the slope. The mules continued to pull and little by little the ambulance rose out of the drainage ditch until finally it was back on the road.

Fernando let out a loud cheer of delight and slapped Dani on the back. The Captain went over and shook hands with the mule driver.

"*Gracias amigo*," he said.

"My pleasure Comrade Captain."

"Let's get back to the castle shall we? Aren't you anxious to find out if it's a boy or a girl?"

"I don't mind what it is, as long as it's healthy."

They left Fernando and Paco to change the punctured tyre and led the mules back along the road to the village. Back up at the castle they found Elizabeth washing her hands with water from an earthenware jug.

"You have a beautiful baby daughter," she told the man.

"Thank you," he said and he grabbed the nurse to him and hugged her tightly for all he was worth. "Tell me your name and I will call my daughter after you."

"Elizabeth," she told him.

"Then my daughter's name is Elizabeth," decided the man triumphantly. "Can I see them?"

"Yes, they're resting but doing fine. You need to keep them warm tonight."

"I'll make a fire," called out the man and he went over to where his little son was kneeling on the ground looking at his mother and his new baby sister wrapped together in blankets.

"Let's get going," whispered Dani to Elizabeth and they left the family alone, walking away from the ruined castle and back through the abandoned village.

"Tell me," said Dani as they left the village, "was that the first time you've helped give birth to a child?"

"There weren't many pregnant wounded soldiers in Madrid," she told him.

When they got back to the lorry they found Paco and Fernando waiting impatiently. The punctured tyre was changed and they were ready to go.

Now they would have to pray that they didn't get another puncture, since they had used the only spare. It was just one more thing for Dani to worry about.

Paco put his foot down to try to make up some lost time, but it wasn't easy to drive the heavy lorry very fast along the twisting pot-holed track. They stopped briefly by a bridge over a fast-running mountain stream to fill up with water and check that the radiator was still functioning properly and then they were off once again forging between mountains. It was a calm and peaceful night and it would have been easy to forget that there was still a war on. Dani closed his eyes and let his head bob slightly from side to side with the rhythm of the lorry's movements.

Paco kept quiet and let the Captain doze. Besides, he was busy with his own thoughts. Up until now this young Captain had been lucky, but there would come a time when his luck would run out and he would get them all killed. The more he thought about it, the more Paco began to realize that he had to start thinking about his own safety and his own future. If they were to reach Alicante successfully then possibly Dani would be offered a place on a ship to safety, but what would happen to the poor old driver? Maybe Dani had already been offered an escape as a way of getting him to accept this mission in the first place. That had to be it. And so Dani and the nurse and possibly Fernando too would all get onto a ship bound for safety and he would be left with a worthless American ambulance and a few bullets for his gun so that he could go out fighting. Of course he would have to save the last bullet for himself. It wasn't a pleasant future that awaited him. He would have to come up with an escape plan of his own and put it into action before they got to Alicante. He knew that the lorry's secret cargo was the key to everyone else's survival, but he would have to make it the key to his own survival instead.

THIRTEEN

Dani awoke as they crossed a little bridge to skirt around the village of San Clemente. They were about twenty kilometres from joining the main road to Albacete at Minaya and dawn couldn't be far away. Their worst nightmare was going to come true, they were going to be exposed in daylight on the main road into Albacete. The sensible thing to do would be to find somewhere to hide up for the day as they had done during the last two days, but Dani felt that they needed to reach Albacete as soon as possible. In Albacete they would get news of how the war was going, they might be able to get some more petrol and they might be able to find a mechanic who could fix their leaking radiator. Another good thing would be some food and a decent place to rest for a while without having to be on maximum alert.

When they joined the main highroad they were once again surrounded by refugees. Some had been walking all night by the look of them, their faces tired and ghostly-white, others had rested for a while and got an early start. There were little carts pulled by mules piled high with items of furniture that for some reason people thought would be useful to them but all they did was slow down their escape and block up the road. The lorry slowed to a crawl and Paco became extremely agitated. People seemed not to hear the lorry approaching or perhaps they just didn't care anymore. The sky began to lighten as they saw the town of La Roda up ahead, the tall tower of the church reaching skywards. They passed another broken down windmill and then came upon a group of soldiers sitting by the roadside. Hearing the ambulance they got to their feet and stood in the road. One of them held up a hand and with a curse Paco brought the lorry to a halt.

"Don't shoot anyone unless I tell you to," whispered Dani. Paco gave him a look that seemed to say I'll shoot who I like and that might include you. Dani wound down his window to talk to the soldiers. These weren't part of a local militia or forgotten boy soldiers left along the retreat, these were real Republican troops sent out from Albacete.

"Buenos días Comrade Captain," said the soldier who seemed to be in charge of the little group raising his clenched fist in salute.

"Buenos días," replied Dani.

"What's your business?"

"Here are my orders," Dani told him reaching slowly and carefully into his pocket. The man studied the papers for a couple of minutes. Whether he really cared what the orders said at this stage of a lost war or whether he was just going through the motions in front of the others Dani couldn't tell. Eventually the soldier handed the papers back to Dani.

"I wouldn't hang around in Albacete too long Comrade Captain if I were you," laughed the man.

"Why is that comrade?"

"Everyone there is desperately trying to save themselves. The city is preparing to surrender and anything with wheels has already left."

"The same as in Madrid. Well, we'd better get going I wouldn't want Albacete to surrender before we get there. Good luck comrade. Viva la República!"

"Viva la República!" responded the guard. As the lorry started off again the group of soldiers stood aside and made the clenched fist salute. What would happen to these poor fellows when the Fascists arrived? Perhaps they naively assumed that they would simply be allowed to return to their villages and resume the lives they had had before the war. Dani knew that that would not be the case. He knew well enough that when the Rebels entered a town, however insignificant, there would be a furious hunt for Reds. Anyone who held a grudge against a neighbour would be able to come forward and denounce them as a communist and that person would be taken away and never seen again. Cousins would give up cousins, friends would murder friends. Defeat brought out the worst in people, and of course everyone wanted to prove their loyalty to the new regime in any way they could.

*

The first rays of light coming through the window played across Captain Roberto Ruiz Roman's face. He was instantly awake. He sat up and rubbed his eyes. He would just have a quick wash and then go out into the town to see if the field telephone was connected yet. It was frustrating for him not to be in touch with the airfield to be able to know if the planes he had up searching had spotted anything. He also wanted to pass on the new information that the lorry they were looking for was an ambulance. He swung his legs off the bed and his feet landed on the body of the woman he had killed during the night. He couldn't even remember doing it. He looked down at her startled white face the eyes still open, a halo of blood around her on the floor. Carefully he got up from his bed and went across to the dressing table where there was a basin of cold water. He splashed some into his eyes and rubbed his face with his hands before drying them on a little towel. Then he left the room and the dead woman behind him.

He found his driver curled up in the back of the staff car fast asleep. He decided not to wake him just yet as he wanted to see the group commander about the telephone situation and so he walked along the tree-lined street towards the centre of the village. There were soldiers everywhere. Sleeping in doorways and on balconies, even curled up in the street in small groups under the trees.

Roberto came to the little inn where the group headquarters had been set up for the night. There was a sentry on guard leaning lazily against the door frame. Hearing someone approach he straightened himself up, and seeing the Captain gave the fascist salute. Roberto ignored the man on guard and went inside to find the group commander. He had half expected to be told that he was still in bed asleep, but Roberto found him sitting at a wooden table having an early breakfast.

"Good morning Captain," said the Commander, "please join me for breakfast?"

"Thank you," said Roberto and he sat down opposite the other man.

"There's no telephone connection at the moment I'm afraid. I've got someone working on it and there should be some good news in an hour or so."

"When will you push on with the advance?"

"Well, I have to speak to my General and ask him what I should do. I expect we'll set off again around mid-morning."

"Can't you leave any sooner?"

"I have to wait for my orders Captain and my men have to be fed. The canteen trucks are on their way and we're waiting for ammunition too."

"Maybe I should set off on my own."

"Only if you want to be killed at the first roadblock you come to. You'd be surprised at just how many of these Reds want to go down fighting. I lost a lot of men yesterday I expect to lose a lot more today. Maybe the Republic will make its last stand in Albacete, who knows?"

"Looks like I'm going to be stuck here for a while then," moaned Roberto. He helped himself to a bread roll and chewed it slowly. A soldier appeared with a cup of something hot that he said was coffee but which when the Captain tried it tasted like warm piss. He just hoped that those bastard airmen had gone up again at first light. He would have their squadron leader shot if they hadn't.

*

For the third day running the pilot was up searching. He had seen a black staff car the previous day, he had seen carts piled high with everything you could imagine being pulled by any beast with four legs and he had seen the people, thousands of them. On the first afternoon, not too far from Madrid, he had come across an open troop carrier heading away from the fallen capital, and although he knew it was not the lorry he was searching for he attacked it anyway. Now his head ached from lack of sleep and the constant searching of moving shapes in the distance. Today they were even further from base and he was watching his fuel gauge carefully, he didn't want to have to perform a forced landing in enemy territory at this late stage of the war. He had been told to concentrate his efforts on the stretch of road leading into Albacete and he was worried about getting too close to the city itself in case there were still organised air defences there. He had already flown over the sierras and was now over the flat plains of La Mancha with its dry low landscape and broken windmills. In the distance he saw a small town hugging the plain in an embrace that had lasted for centuries, and he swooped lower to get a better view. Maybe this mysterious lorry was parked up in the town somewhere.

On the outskirts, a group of ragged soldiers who were sitting by the roadside got to their feet and fired their rifles off at him as he flew overhead. They must have known they had little or no chance of hitting him, but it was what they thought they ought to do. The pilot should have ignored them they were no threat to him or anyone else. They were just waiting at the roadside to surrender their weapons to the first Nationalist troops that came along, but for some reason best known to himself, he decided to turn and shoot at them. He banked his plane low over the first houses of the town and turned back to where he had come from, keeping down as low as he dared. The soldiers saw the plane returning and raised their rifles to fire once more. At the moment they started shooting the pilot opened up with his machine gun, scattering the group of soldiers and all the refugees around them.

One of the soldiers had fallen dead in the road and another was down on all fours coughing blood into the dust. The pilot wheeled away and climbed turning in a wide circle to then swoop back down upon the road. There were people running in all directions now, women dragging their children by the hand, old men hobbling away into the fields as fast as they could go their old wives tumbling into ditches. The pilot looked for the soldiers again and saw that they were no longer in a group instead it was every man for himself. He saw a couple of them running back along the road towards the town hoping to escape that way. He lined them up in his sights and swooped after them, whooping with delight as his machine gun cut them down. He thought about turning and making another pass, but reluctantly decided to use his last remaining minutes of fuel to continue on as close to Albacete as he dared. If he could find the needle in the haystack on this sortie he wouldn't have to fly another one in the afternoon.

He flew low over the town of La Roda, so low that his undercarriage almost brushed the top of the church tower, but he couldn't see anything of interest in the streets below. There were people milling around no doubt trying to decide whether to stay or go and some stood and peered up at him, perhaps the first enemy plane they had ever seen. There would be some who now had had their minds made up and would be racing to get their families packed and on the road. Was there some sort of forlorn hope that their provincial capital would somehow be able to resist the fascist war machine where the great cities of Bilbao, Barcelona and Madrid had failed?

The pilot flew on over the little village of La Gineta to within less than twenty kilometres of Albacete. He checked his fuel gauge for the hundredth time and was relieved to see that he was going to have to turn back within the next few minutes. When he got back to the airfield he could have a wash and get something to eat and maybe a quick nap before they sent him out again. There was always the hope that one of the other planes that had been sent out had got lucky and then he wouldn't have to go up again.

Just before the final stretch of road into Albacete, there was a small collection of farm buildings huddled together. All of a sudden the pilot did a double take, there passing between the low buildings that straddled the road was a slow-moving lorry. He went down for a closer look his heart suddenly beating with excitement. He overshot the lorry at the lowest height he dared to fly and saw that it had a red cross painted on its roof. He pulled the plane up to think about what he had seen. No one had told him that he was hunting for an ambulance. Still, what better way to disguise something that was really important? Could this be what he had been sent to find? It was definitely worth another look he decided.

FOURTEEN

Dani had just been thinking that their luck was going to hold and that they would be able to reach Albacete safely, when the Rebel plane passed directly over them its engine booming in their ears. Paco reacted quickly, slamming on the brakes and pulling the ambulance off the road and into a farmyard. There was nowhere to hide the lorry but he brought it to a standstill as close to an old stable as he could, and then he had his door open and was running to the low stone building for cover. Dani followed him out of the cab and ran to the back of the ambulance shouting for the other two to get out as quickly as possible. Fernando appeared at the tailgate and seeing the look of panic on his friend's face jumped down to the ground.

"There's a plane coming," shouted Dani at Elizabeth who was still at the back wrapped up in blankets. She jumped to her feet and scampered to get out as fast as she could. The noise of the returning aircraft filled their ears getting deafeningly close. At any moment Dani expected to hear the rattle of its machine gun and to feel the bullets swarming like angry bees all around them. Elizabeth jumped into the arms of the two soldiers just as the pilot was about to fire his machine gun. Suddenly, seeing a woman in a nurse's uniform made him hesitate and then the moment had gone and he was flying away again. Dani, Fernando and Elizabeth reached the stables and threw themselves to the ground panting for breath.

The pilot glanced again at his fuel gauge and knew it was time to head back to base, besides if there was a nurse then it was probably a real ambulance. He laughed insanely to himself at the thought of the fright that he had just given some poor nurse. Well, it was her fault for being on the wrong side in this stupid war. The excitement over, his mind wandered back to thoughts of a rest as his plane wandered back towards the sierras.

*

At last the Commander of the Nationalist's most advanced troops finished his phone conversation with his distant headquarters. Getting the phone link had taken longer than expected, but now he had orders to press on with all possible haste and he set off to find his company captains and to get them to ready their squads for departure. The troop

91

carriers were being refuelled and ammunition was being passed around to those who needed it. It was going to be another long day this time across the plains of La Mancha. He hoped that none of his men would go mad and start attacking windmills.

Roberto grabbed the field telephone before anyone else could and waited impatiently to be put through to the airbase at Cuatro Vientos. He had been fuming at the hours of delay and was about ready to explode. He hoped to god that there was good news from the base. Eventually he got to speak to the squadron leader who informed him that all the planes had now returned from their morning sorties and that there was nothing special to report. When the captain informed the squadron leader of the possibility that the lorry they were searching for might be disguised as an ambulance the line suddenly went silent. For a second or two Roberto thought he had been cut off, god knows it wouldn't have been the first time in this bloody war, but he could still hear the man at the other end breathing raggedly.

Although the Captain was a long way away, the Squadron Leader still feared his wrath. He swallowed hard and informed him that one of his pilots had almost attacked an ambulance just a few kilometres away from Albacete, but had seen a nurse getting out of the back and assumed it was a genuine medical vehicle. Roberto exploded, cursing the man and every generation of his family as far back as he could imagine, and then he wanted the pilot taken out and shot on the runway as an example to the other members of the squadron. How could they let this happen? How useless was it possible for a bunch of loony fliers to be? If they let this prize get away General Franco himself would hear about it.

The Squadron Leader let the distant Captain rage on until he had run out of steam and then promised he would have his aircraft back up as soon as they were refuelled and the pilots rested. This annoyed Roberto all over again and he shouted that they were to get out again immediately, the bastard pilots could rest in hell once he had ripped their useless guts out. He slammed the phone down and went outside. He would just have to hope that the ground troops made swift progress over the coming hours and that Albacete would be captured before nightfall. Back in the street seeing groups of soldiers still milling around he doubted that they would get very far at all. He strode off in a simmering fury to find his driver. He would take advantage of the chance to refuel here and save the spare cans of petrol for another time. Once this mission was finished he would need enough fuel to be able to get back to Madrid.

*

Dani was still a little shaken from the sudden episode with the plane. It had appeared from nowhere and it was only Paco's quick thinking that had saved them. He still couldn't decide why the pilot hadn't opened fire. Perhaps the man had fallen for the ambulance guise which Dani had never thought would fool anyone. Whatever the reason, they were now approaching Albacete and some sort of relative safety and he felt greatly relieved.

Just outside the city they stopped at a system of trenches and high stone walls swarming with soldiers. Dani explained that they had orders to reach Alicante and that they were transporting a very important cargo. No one seemed to care too much about them entering the city and the Captain in command of the outer defences had more important things to worry about and so they were quickly allowed to pass into Albacete. Dani and Fernando had been there before, but they weren't prepared for how the city had changed. It had been bombed from the air on several occasions and many of its buildings lay in ruins. Once it had been the centre of the expectations of the International Brigades and the streets had hummed with the sounds of their enthusiastic marching and singing, but now there were no more *brigadistas*, those who had not been fed to the Nationalist machine guns had been sent back home to save them from having to witness the final death of the Republic.

Albacete was a tragic and pathetic sight. There were no ordinary people visible, just ragged soldiers picking their way through the ruins moving from one gun post to the next. Some were sharing out the final cases of ammunition, some trying to scrounge a bit of food or a cigarette, the political commissars trying impossibly to raise the moral of these oft defeated men for one last stand.

Paco parked the ambulance in a little square not too far from the centre and the four of them got out. They stood looking around at the dilapidated buildings, wondering what it must have been like to live in this place through the war. In 1936, at the start of the war, Albacete had been taken by Rebel civil guards but had then been recaptured by

Republican forces at the end of July 1936. It became the Headquarters for the thousands of volunteers of the International Brigades because of its excellent communication links with the Mediterranean ports.

In the corner of the square was a sand-bagged anti-aircraft gun position, its crew warming themselves after a cold night, sitting in the sun. Paco went over to speak to them.

"The Headquarters is at the Gran Hotel, it's not far from here," the driver informed them when he came back.

"We know it don't we Nando," said Dani, "it's where the Internationals had their High Command."

"Yes, I remember, nice place."

"I'll stay here with the lorry," said Paco, "it's as good a place as any. Those comrades reckon they should be fed sometime this morning, so I'm going to hang about for that."

"Sounds good to me too," decided Fernando.

"Okay, you stay here. I'll take Elizabeth to the Hotel and see if I can find her somewhere to rest for the day. Maybe I can find out if the Rebels have captured Alicante or not."

Dani and Elizabeth set off through the shattered streets of the city towards the Plaza Altozano where the Gran Hotel was. The narrow streets were blocked at regular intervals by makeshift barricades made from the bricks of bombed-out buildings and sandbags. Soldiers sat behind them on broken chairs stolen from the cafés and restaurants and dozed in the sunshine. They soon became alert when they saw Elizabeth and some called out to her that they were in need of special medical attention, others whistled, some just stared with open mouths. How could they possibly be seeing a beautiful woman in the midst of this miasma of hopelessness? For some, she would be the last woman they would ever see, just as she had been for many dying men back in Madrid.

They found the Gran Hotel still resplendent with its balustrades and tiny curved balconies and impressive stonework, and a little out of place in such a war zone. Its beautiful façade was a distant memory of better turn of the century times. A bomb had landed in the little garden in the square and blown away the trees and benches, but the hotel was as yet unscathed. There were a pair of soldiers on idle guard at the entrance to the hotel and they gave the clenched fist salute as Dani and Elizabeth walked past them into the hotel foyer.

Inside there was chaos. The foyer was covered with stray pieces of paper and there were boxes full of paperwork and more being added to them by a team of administration staff who were clearing out the files. Everything relating to the Republic in Albacete was going to be taken out into the square and burnt before it could fall into enemy hands and be used for retributions. Here were the names and passport details of all the members of the International Brigades, thousands of them, as well as details of all those who were members of the local communist party and the socialist trades unions. There were probably also records of the hundreds of political assassinations that had taken place in reprisal for the Rebel uprising at the beginning of the war. There were plenty of people in Albacete with blood on their hands, and there would be plenty more before this whole thing was over.

Dani spoke to a young soldier seated behind a desk and was directed up to the first floor where he would find someone who might be prepared to listen to him. They climbed the ornate staircase and eventually found the office of a soldier who looked like he might be in charge. Dani gave the clenched fist salute and showed his orders. The man glanced at the papers but didn't really care enough to read them. The whole Republic was going to hell.

"What can I do for you?" asked the man.

"Well, I wondered if there might be a spare room here at the hotel where this English nurse could rest for a few hours, you know, maybe have a wash. We've been travelling all night. Some food would be nice too if there's any going spare."

"There's a dining room down in the basement there's normally some sort of soup on the go, help yourselves. There are rooms on the top two floors, people come and go, I dare say a few have gone for good, go have a look after you've eaten."

"Thank you comrade, *viva la República!*" said Dani.

"Sure," replied the man and he dismissed them with a little wave of his hand and went back to more important things like how to surrender a city without getting all its inhabitants slaughtered and all his soldiers shot without trial.

Down in the basement they were amazed that the dining room still had a good compliment of wooden tables and chairs and even a waiter ceremoniously carrying bowls of soup out from the kitchen.

"Good morning comrades," said the waiter cheerfully almost as if they were normal guests in normal times.

"What's on the menu comrade?" asked Dani.

"On the menu today we have soup, the same as every day."

"Two bowls of soup then if there are none of Dr Negrín's little brown pills." The man gave a short laugh and went off to the kitchen.

"What are Dr Negrín's little brown pills?" Elizabeth whispered.

"That's what we call lentils. For most people during this war, on our side at least, it was the best sort of meal they could hope for."

The waiter returned with the soup in beautiful china bowls and some silver spoons from the hotel's finest service.

"It isn't often these days that our dining room is graced by such a beautiful being as your *señora*," the waiter said by way of explanation for such luxury. He placed a small loaf of bread at Elizabeth's elbow. "You might want to take the bread with you for another occasion," he whispered, "that's all I have. Tomorrow, if we're still alive, we'll be eating fascist bread."

"*Gracias*," said Elizabeth giving the man a smile. Dani tasted the soup with his silver spoon and wished it had been more in keeping with their surroundings. Any bones that had once been in the pot must have been boiled clear away and apart from water the soup had only the merest hint of a distant vegetable or two and a slight pinch of salt.

"Nice soup," laughed Elizabeth.

"Yes, *no está mal*," agreed Dani.

When they had finished, Elizabeth wrapped the bread in her spare blouse and put it into her bag for safe-keeping. If Fernando and Paco hadn't managed to get anything to eat then she would give it to them, otherwise it would be divided into four at their next shared mealtime. She was glad to have something to be able to contribute.

They climbed the splendid staircase once more, this time up to the top floor, Dani thought there were more likely to be empty rooms up there out of the way. They tried a few doors until eventually they found one that opened. The room was dark with the shutters closed and Elizabeth went over to the window to open them. As the sunlight flooded in they found a grand bed with a mattress but no sheets or blankets. On the sideboard was a large china bowl of clean water the previous occupant hadn't thought to use.

"This will do Dani," said the nurse.

"Good, I'll go back to the square with the others, I'll come back for you in a few hours."

"Don't go Dani, I don't want to be here alone."

"You'll be all right. Just keep the door locked and don't open it to anyone who doesn't speak English," he laughed.

"No, please, I won't be able to sleep if I'm alone." Dani looked around for chair but there wasn't one. He looked at Elizabeth.

"Just lie on the bed with me," she whispered, "you need to rest too."

"Maybe just for a little while then," he decided.

"Good. Just wait outside whilst I have a wash and get changed."

When he was allowed back into the room Dani washed his face and took off his jacket and his boots and then rather awkwardly climbed onto the bed beside the nurse. He lay on his back and Elizabeth put her head on his chest as there was no pillow and closed her eyes listening to his heartbeat. Dani stroked her hair and waited for her to fall asleep, but he hadn't counted on just how exhausted he was himself, and within minutes they were both dead to the world.

FIFTEEN

The General had been summoned onboard the Mexican ship that had been waiting in the harbour for him. The Captain was getting anxious. He didn't want to be anywhere near Alicante when the Rebels arrived, they might impound his vessel as war booty and have the whole crew shot. Also, there were now hundreds of people milling around the docks area desperate to board a ship to anywhere, and rumour had it that there were thousands more on the way. Discipline was just about still under control but in the few final hours it might all go to hell.

The General had promised a large sum of money to reserve a space in the ship's cargo hold and the Captain had agreed to delay sailing until whatever the General wanted to take with him to Mexico had arrived. However, he couldn't delay much longer without putting his ship and her crew in very grave danger.

"My dear General," smiled the Captain shaking the other man's podgy hand. "I need to know how much longer I'm expected to wait."

"I was hoping that the lorry from Madrid would arrive in the night, but it hasn't done so. It must have been delayed slightly. I'm sure it will arrive tonight."

"Tonight? I'm not sure if I can wait any longer. I was hoping to set sail on the tide this evening. It's getting a little too dangerous for us here."

"You must give me until tomorrow morning. I'm paying you a lot of money. If you leave without me then you get nothing."

"Maybe you're not paying me enough," stated the Captain, "I'm sure there must be someone else here who'll pay me the same amount to save their skin. Maybe there are people willing to pay a bit more. What do you think?"

"I'll pay you double," said the General.

"Double? Really?"

"Yes, but you must give me until tomorrow morning." The Captain thought about it for a moment.

"Okay General, you've got yourself a deal. But the tide tomorrow is at twelve noon, and this ship sails then, with or without your special cargo."

"It'll be here, trust me."

"Good. We sail tomorrow. I'll tell my crew They're all starting to get a bit nervous." The two men shook hands and the General left the ship. By the time he was down the gangplank and back on dry land he was sweating like a pig. Being as fat and as out of condition as he was it didn't take much to make him sweat, but the thought that he might lose his place on the ship was really getting to him, add to that the heat of the Mediterranean after a winter holed up in a cellar in freezing Madrid and anyone would be sweating. The fact that he had just had to offer the Mexican Captain double money didn't bother him it was just peanuts compared to what was at stake. Maybe he would shoot the man when they reached Mexico rather than pay him. That thought cheered the fat general up a bit as he walked out of the docks towards the market cleaning the sweat off his tiny round glasses.

*

Captain Roberto was relieved to be on the move once more. They were pushing ahead across the plains of La Mancha without meeting much resistance. At most of the tiny villages the people stayed indoors hoping that the Rebel army would just pass through and leave them alone. If the soldiers were thirsty then they might break down a farmhouse door and demand water, but other than that their orders were to press on towards Albacete. The Advanced Commander wanted to lay siege to the city before nightfall if possible. He hoped that when they saw the first Nationalist troops arrive and felt the heat from their bombardment that the defenders would surrender. Franco had given orders that there were to be no deals, unconditional surrender was the only thing to be accepted. The Commander's job was to take the surrender and then move on to Alicante with all possible haste. The Generalisimo wanted the Republic's Mediterranean ports captured as soon as possible so that there would be no mass evacuation. Another advanced group was already pressing forward towards Valencia where the Republican Government had been installed since the attack on Madrid in 1936.

Everything was going well until they came to the town of Belmonte and found its population and those of the surrounding villages holed up in the magnificent fifteenth century castle. There were no real soldiers present since these had been pulled back to defend Albacete and the castle walls and turrets were manned by members of the local militias and by farmers with a mad collection of ancient hunting weapons.

The first troops to approach were greeted by a hail of bullets and strange projectiles from the castle's outer walls, but the defenders in their enthusiasm had fired too soon, before the attackers were in range, and so all surprise was lost. The Commander called a halt and waited for the heavy guns to be brought up. He didn't want to waste time in this insignificant place, but he couldn't very well leave a fully-defended castle behind. He imagined the other group taking Valencia with him still stuck here sitting on the plain.

Roberto saw the castle up ahead and cursed. There was nothing he could do except pace up and down the road alongside his parked car mumbling in frustration. If they didn't get to Albacete soon he would lose any chance of capturing the lorry he had chased all this way. He decided that the moment Albacete was taken he would race ahead on his own towards Alicante. If the lorry reached the port before him then its cargo would be on a ship and sailing off to safety and he would have failed for the first time in his military career. He wasn't about to let that happen. He hoped that when the big guns arrived the Commander would blow a hole in the castle walls and send his troops in. Better still, pound the castle to smithereens and kill everyone inside, what did he care if it was one of the most beautiful castles in Spain or that it had belonged to the Condesa de Teba, Eugenia de Montijo, who was married to Napoleon III of France?

Roberto's driver offered the Captain a cigarette to try to calm him down a bit, to be honest when he was in a rage the man scared him to death. He wasn't sure that their being on the same side would mean much if the Captain blew his top. So Roberto and his driver sat on the bonnet of their little car and smoked foul cigarettes and waited for something to happen.

It was early afternoon before the big guns arrived pulled by huge straining lorries. They were Italian guns and had already been used to good effect against more important targets than this. The defenders in their castle saw the guns and saw the arrival of more and more troops by the hour and rightly decided that further resistance would be futile. A delegation was sent out from the fortress under a flag of truce to negotiate the surrender, only to be told that there would be no negotiations. The Commander gave them one hour to open the gates of the castle and come out or he would commence shelling.

After about forty-five minutes the townspeople surrendered and the gates of the fortress were thrown open. The men filed out with their hands in the air having left their weapons inside. Relieved that it was all over, the Commander ordered a small detachment of his infantry to remain behind and restore order whilst the rest of his force and the big Italian guns set off once more for Albacete. No one was happier with the conclusion of the siege than Roberto, and even as the first volley of shots from the firing squad was ringing out across the plains of La Mancha he was in his car ready to follow as close to the front of the advance as his driver dared.

*

Dani awoke suddenly to find Elizabeth's face just a few inches from his own. It took him a second or two to work out what he was doing at such close quarters with the beautiful English nurse, and then he smiled up at her.

"Hi there sleepy head," she whispered.

"Hi. What were you doing?"

"I was just watching you sleep. You looked like a little boy."

"What time is it?"

"I don't know, but we must have been asleep for several hours I would think."

"We'd better get back to the others they'll be worried about us."

They left the surreal calm of the Gran Hotel in the Plaza Altozano and headed back to where the lorry was parked. Once more they passed through the side-street barricades to the appreciative comments of the soldiers who were waiting there to die. Elizabeth was glad she was with Dani.

The lorry was just where they had left it and Paco was asleep in the cab. Fernando was nowhere to be seen, no doubt off trying to scrounge some food or wine. They sat in the lorry's growing shadow on a piece of the pavement that hadn't yet been blown up and waited for Fernando to return.

Suddenly, from away in the distance Dani heard the familiar sound of approaching planes. These were unmistakeably the heavier engines of bombers. The Captain jumped up and dashed to the cab of the ambulance to wake the sleeping driver.

"Quick, Paco, we've got to get the lorry under cover there are bombers coming." Paco didn't waste any time and quickly started up the engine. Dani pointed to some high arches across the square that formed a covered walkway in front of what must once have been shops and cafés and Paco put the motor into gear and they began to cross the square. Somewhere not too far away they heard the rumble of the first exploding bombs and Dani knew it would be touch and go as to whether they made it to shelter in time or not. The antiaircraft gun in the square sprang to life to offer a warning that the bombers were now in full view. A daylight raid was a clear way of showing the defenders of Albacete that their attackers had nothing to fear and that further resistance was futile.

Paco squeezed the lorry into an archway between two columns and slammed on the brakes. He and Dani jumped from the cab and dived under the ambulance only for Dani to peer out and see Elizabeth still running about half way across the square. He was about to go and get her when he saw Fernando emerge from a side street. Fernando sprinted over to Elizabeth and grabbed her by the waist. He hoisted her up into the air and started to run with her towards the shelter of the arches.

A bomb exploded at the entrance to the square where the lorry had been parked barely minutes before, blowing the corner of a building to pieces. Fernando arrived just in time, as a second bomb blew a hole in the middle of the square, he shoved Elizabeth under the lorry and then dived under himself panting for breath. The third bomb scored a direct hit on the antiaircraft battery.

How long the raid lasted it was difficult to tell. For those on the receiving end it seemed like hours but it was probably only a few minutes before the Italian bombers completed their run and turned back to base. They would refuel and try to do a second run before nightfall or they might be sent to bomb Alicante in the twilight, just to let the people there know that their time was coming soon.

When they were sure that the bombers were gone the four of them crawled out from under the lorry dusting themselves off. It had been a close thing. Elizabeth was understandably a bit shaken, but she wiped the tears from her eyes and went over to see if there was anything she could do for the antiaircraft gun crew. Dani followed her over.   When they got there all that remained were a few split sandbags and a man's headless torso trapped underneath the mangled barrel of the gun. The nurse put her hand over her mouth and backed away. Dani led her back to the lorry by the arm. The other two were calmly smoking cigarettes. Once again she asked herself why on earth had she wanted to come to this foreign war? They sat under the arches waiting for the sun to go down hoping that the bombers wouldn't return. The thing that was worrying Dani the most was the fact that all the petrol they had was what was in the tank. He hadn't mentioned it to Elizabeth, but Fernando had spent most of the day trying to get his hands on some, but there wasn't a drop to be found.

SIXTEEN

Daylight was beginning to fade as the Nationalist advance swept into La Roda just forty kilometres short of Albacete. The troops were tired and it was decided to leave the attack on Albacete for first light. Roberto had known that this was going to happen. As soon as they had encountered a little resistance on the edge of town and waited for a few stray Republican soldiers to be cleared away he had known that the Commander would call a halt. There was no point complaining, it wasn't going to change anything. Instead he and his driver stood beside their car looking at a map.

Roberto's plan was to try to bypass Albacete during the night and catch up with the lorry on the road. It would mean a large detour and a lot of driving, mostly on small unmade roads, but it had the advantage of avoiding any major villages. Of course once they rejoined the main road they would be ahead of the advance and therefore behind enemy lines. He hoped they would catch up with the lorry as it struggled down through the sierras towards the coastal shelf. It was a dangerous strategy, but the only one that Roberto had left open to him. If he waited another day for the fall of Albacete then his mission was doomed to end in failure.

His driver was not pleased. They had been on the move all day and now the plan was to drive through the night. Seeing the man's obvious disapproval the Captain agreed to share the driving and let his driver rest from time to time. Before setting off they would wash and change clothes, get something to eat and fill the car with petrol. If they didn't catch the lorry within the next few hours then they would be heading back to Madrid empty-handed, to face the wrath of General Franco himself.

*

At dusk Paco filled the lorry's ailing radiator with water and declared that they were ready to go. He knew they didn't have enough fuel to make it to Alicante, but his plans didn't call for that eventuality anyway. Dani was also apprehensive about the petrol situation but still held out some hope that what they had in the tank would get them to their destination. It had to. They had no way of refuelling on route.

The air raid had left Albacete in turmoil. Soldiers were standing in small groups asking each other what they ought to do, should they stay and fight and die, should they stay and surrender or should they flee for the coast? Most of the barricades were no longer manned. Paco drove the lorry carefully around the new debris caused by the Italian bombers, and on every street corner soldiers called out to be allowed to go with them thinking that in an ambulance they might be safe. Some offered up their wounded comrades for transportation to the coast. Paco cursed as the lorry jolted over a dead body lying in the street that he hadn't been able to avoid.

Eventually they were free of the shabby ruins of Albacete and could get on towards Alicante. They wouldn't hug the back roads now, their situation called for speed more than safety. Dani knew that it would only be a matter of hours before they were swallowed up by the Nationalist advance. There was nothing that was going to stop it. He had seen the despair in Albacete and he knew that the city's resistance wouldn't last very long. And of course people, normal people, wanted the war to be over. They were tired of the killing and the hunger and the uncertainty. Everyone wanted things to return to normal, although of course that was never going to happen. All over the shrinking Republican zone soldiers were abandoning their last posts and setting off on foot for home.

They drove past the airfield at Los Llanos and saw the burning wrecks of buildings and planes and realised that rather than returning to bomb the city, the Italians had unleashed their second attack on the airbase. Once again the road was crowded with refugees heads bowed, walking, just trying to get as much distance as possible away from the city.

The first place they came to was the village of Chinchilla de Monte-Aragón, a group of tiny houses clustered around the foot of a large outcrop of rock, upon which stood the castle. In the distance just beneath the moon they were able to make out the peaks of the distant sierras from which they would descend down towards the coast.

*

Roberto was driving and driving fast, charging along a back road to the north of Albacete. He had agreed to take the first turn at the wheel and incredibly the other man was curled up asleep on the back seat of the car. He didn't even stir when they took a sharp bend almost flat out in a shower of gravel and dirt. That was what fatigue could do to a man in a war. Perhaps, when this was over he would give his driver a couple of days' leave whilst he interrogated a few Reds in Madrid. It annoyed him to have to let other people do his job. He hoped they weren't being too lenient.

Roberto remembered when he had been in Madrid before the war, a young cadet in a stiff new uniform taking his first leave from the officer training school. He had gone with a few other young soldiers to the Puerta del Sol. They had had a glass of wine in a dirty bar and then gone to a small backstreet theatre. About half way through the dreadful performance Roberto's companions decided that the bar was a lot more entertaining than the play, but Roberto decided to stay. There was a beautiful young actress playing a secondary role and he couldn't take his eyes off her. He was transfixed. Never in his life had he noticed a woman before, the only thing that had ever seemed important to him was to become a soldier like his father before him. And yet, here in this dimly lit theatre he was unexpectedly struck by the beauty of this girl.

The play toiled on towards its fanciful conclusion and Roberto sat there staring. When the girl spoke, her eyes lowered with shyness, it was as if she was speaking just to him and the other spectators in the theatre simply vanished. When the play finished and the players took their bows Roberto stood and applauded long and hard, doubly so when the girl came to the edge of the stage, so much so that the other people in the audience began to look at him in a strange manner. Roberto didn't care.

When the lights came on he dashed out into the street to find a flower seller and purchased some beautiful white lilies. Their petals were as white and delicate as the girl's skin and he thought that they would be perfect for her. Back at the theatre he waited for the young actress to emerge from the stage door. He waited for what seemed like forever, his heart pounding strangely in his chest, his breathing laboured and ragged.

Eventually, she emerged along with a couple of the other actors. Roberto didn't know what to say and so he just held out the flowers towards her.

"I think you've got an admirer," laughed one of the men. The girl took the flowers from Roberto's shaking hands.

106

"*Gracias*," she said with a little giggle looking at the absurd cadet in his stiff new uniform his face so pale he looked ill.

"Perhaps we could go for a drink?" he managed to say despite the dryness in his throat. She paused just for a second, looked him up and down and gave another giggle.

"I don't think so." She hooked her arm through the arm of her two fellow actors and they set off up the street. Roberto had remained rooted to the spot for a long time, his face purple with rage, his whole body shaking. How dare she just reject him like that, she didn't even know him. Back at the barracks in his bed that night he had dreamt of the girl and in the morning he cursed himself for his stupidity.

What had happened to that actress he wondered. He hoped that she had been killed in an air raid, or better still, that she had been taken prisoner and was waiting in a cell in Madrid and that when he returned he would be able to interrogate her. Guilty or not he would be able to make her confess to any crime he wanted, and when she was completely broken and begged to die he would remind her of how she had treated him that day outside the theatre. Roberto laughed to himself at the thought and thumped the steering wheel with pleasure. The driver slept on in the back not realizing that Roberto almost had the car off the road and into a field as they rounded a bend.

*

Once they were some distance from Albacete the road began to clear of refugees. Most of those who were going to flee had decided to head across country for the sierras, they thought it safer than the road. It was only those who had left it to the last minute to make their decision that had decided that Alicante was the best choice. Anyone with a radio would have heard on Radio Valencia that the Mediterranean ports were already teeming with people and that there were no boats to take them anywhere. With the winter behind them there would be hope for people to survive for a few weeks up in the mountains and then return to their homes when things had returned to some sort of normal. No one could have imagined that the Nationalists would send the Civil Guard up into the sierras to hunt down those who had fled and shoot them like stray dogs.

Paco stopped the lorry alongside a reservoir. They had done about fifty kilometres from Albacete and the petrol gauge was hovering close to empty, how much farther they could go he wasn't sure, but this desolate place in the middle of nowhere seemed the perfect spot for what he had planned. As the lorry came to a standstill the driver pulled out a pistol and pointed it straight at Dani's face.

"What the fuck is this?" Dani demanded.

"This comrade Captain is as far as you go."

"What are you talking about Paco?"

"I've been giving it some serious thought these last twenty-four hours. If we get to Alicante then everyone gets a good old slap on the back. You get a fucking medal and the General finds everyone a place on a ship to somewhere nice. But what about me? Not the poor bloody driver, no, I'll just get left behind to face a fascist firing squad."

"You don't know that. I'm sure the General will be equally grateful to all of us."

"Maybe he will, maybe we'll all be for the firing squad. But I'm not about to take any chances."

"You can't betray us to the enemy Paco. Not after everything that we've been through to get this far."

"I have no choice. Besides, we're almost out of petrol. This lorry isn't taking us much farther."

"Maybe we can get some fuel in the next town," said Dani desperately trying to buy some time in the hope that Fernando would come to see what was going on.

"Whatever this lorry is carrying has got to be important enough for me to be able to save my life by handing it over."

"How can you betray us? How can you betray the Republic in its hour of need?"

"Hasn't everyone betrayed everyone already in this war?" grunted the driver. "Okay, enough stalling, let's get out, very slowly shall we?"

Without taking his eyes off Dani, Paco opened the driver's side door and stepped out of the cab, motioning with the gun for Dani to follow him. Just as the Captain's feet hit the gravel of the roadside Fernando jumped down from the back of the lorry to find out why they had stopped.

108

"Hey, what's going on?" he called out when he saw the driver pointing a gun at Dani. Paco turned and fired at Fernando, the crack of the gun splitting the silence of the night. The bullet thudded into Fernando's left shoulder and knocked him to the ground. He screamed out in pain and Elizabeth screamed from inside the back of the ambulance knowing that something terrible was happening.

"Tell that stupid English bitch to shut up. And tell her that if she shows her face I'll shoot her."

"Let her live Paco please," pleaded Dani, "she's got nothing to do with this."

"Tell her to stay in the back and to keep quiet and I'll think about letting her live, as long as you don't cause me any trouble of course."

"I'll do whatever you say comrade, just don't hurt the girl."

SEVENTEEN

Roberto, still driving like a madman, saw up ahead the point where the track he had taken to bypass Albacete rejoined the main Alicante Highroad. Not too far away he could make out the impressive castle at Chinchilla de Monte-Aragon ghostly in the moonlight, perched on a rocky outcrop looking down on the little houses clustered around it. They would rejoin the main road just past the village which was a relief to Roberto who didn't fancy being a one-man liberation force however small the place might be.

He stopped the car and woke his driver. He wanted to be fresh for when they found the lorry and to be able to fire from the moving car if he needed to. The driver groaned in protest when Roberto opened the rear door and let in the cold night air. They were close to the sierras and the temperature had dropped compared to the plains around Albacete. It wouldn't be long before they were into the mountains and once they were out the other side it would be an easy run down to the coast. He was confident that they would catch up with the lorry as it laboured through the sierras. They had been lucky to elude him for so long, but now their luck was running out.

The driver rubbed the sleep from his face and they set off along the main road, Roberto straining his eyes ahead into the darkness desperate for that first glimpse of the prey they had been pursuing for so long and which he felt was now so near.

*

"Elizabeth," Dani called out, "Don't come out of the lorry."

"What's going on?" she shouted back. Dani thought for a minute and decided that Paco wouldn't understand what he was going to say in English. He just hoped that he wasn't going to get the girl killed.

"Paco has betrayed us. He's shot Fernando and he's going to shoot me too. If you stay inside the lorry you won't come to any harm, do you hear?"

"Dani, no!" wailed the nurse.

"There's a gun in Fernando's kitbag, get it in case you have to defend yourself when the Rebels come."

110

"What are you saying?" demanded Paco annoyed at them speaking in a language he couldn't understand. They thought they were so clever these two with their private whispered conversations and their little knowing looks when they thought no one was watching. But Paco had been watching. Maybe he fancied the girl for himself. Maybe when this was over she would realize that he had done the right thing and be grateful to him.

"I was just telling her that nothing bad would happen to her and that she shouldn't come out."

"Good. Now, let's get your friend down to the lake shall we."

Dani went over to Fernando and looked down at his friend who was groaning and barely conscious a big dark stain spreading from the wound in his left shoulder.

"Oh my god, Nando, it looks like this is the end for us *amigo*," whispered Dani taking his friend's right arm and pulling gently to encourage him to get to his feet. Fernando could only grunt, his teeth gritted against the pain. Slowly he got to his feet. He felt light-headed and would have fallen but for the support of his friend. They had known each other for as long as either could remember, and if they had to die then at least they would die together.

"Down to the water," hissed Paco. He could have just shot them both there by the roadside, but he thought that perhaps when the Nationalists arrived the sight of dead bodies and blood might cause them to shoot first and ask questions later. Paco needed the chance to explain about the special cargo that the lorry was carrying and therefore be able to beg for his life since he had decided to turn it over to them. Dani left the roadside, half-carrying, half-dragging his wounded companion. From the back of the lorry he thought he heard Elizabeth sobbing. It was strange, he hadn't known her for very long but he was suddenly sad at the thought that he would not get to spend more time with her. It was a shame that they hadn't met under better circumstances. He hoped that Paco would be true to his word and let her live, but then again, if she was captured by the fascists god only knew what they might do to her. Paco wouldn't offer her any protection, he was obviously only interested in saving his own skin. A huge frustration welled-up in Dani, but there was nothing he could do about it.

Elizabeth sobbed loudly again, hoping the noise would cover her movements as she rummaged through Fernando's kit bag looking for his pistol. She touched something metallic and drew it out. It was a hunting knife in a leather scabbard. Quickly she lifted her top and thrust the knife down into the waist of her skirt then she went back to looking for the gun.

Dani stumbled a bit as he began to descend the gentle slope down towards the still water of the reservoir. It was difficult to keep his footing in the loose shale. Paco followed a few paces behind them, his gun always pointing down at the two soldiers. He wasn't expecting Dani to go down without a fight, even though he had offered to spare the girl in return for his cooperation. As soon as they were fairly near the water he would shoot the Captain from a distance and then finish off both of them with shots to the head. It reminded him of the time back in his *pueblo* at the beginning of the war when they had taken the priest and his assistant for a *paseo* into the countryside and shot them both.

Elizabeth found the gun in Fernando's kit at last, it was a .38 revolver and although she didn't know much about guns she knew enough from having spent so much time around soldiers that the thing had a safety that needed to be switched in order for it to fire. She found the safety on the side of the gun and pushed it to the only other position it would move to and hoped that now it would fire. She couldn't hear the men nearby so she cautiously stuck her head out of the canvas at the back of the lorry. There they were, going down towards the shore of a lake. Elizabeth climbed quickly down from the lorry, and keeping low, began to descend the slope after the men. She tried not to make a sound but at the same time she knew that if she was going to stand any chance of hitting Paco she would need to be fairly close to him. The men weren't very far from the water's edge now.

"Okay, stop there," called out Paco. Dani froze, so this was the moment. It was strange but he felt almost calm. "I'm sorry it had to come to this comrade," said the driver and he raised his pistol slightly as if to adjust his aim. A shot rang out followed by a female scream. Dani didn't feel the impact of a bullet and suddenly saw that Paco was starting to bleed from a large hole in his chest. The shot man looked up the slope a little way to face his shooter and saw the English nurse falling backwards from the fright of having fired the gun. He managed to squeeze off a shot in her direction before his knees buckled under him and he fell.

"Elizabeth!" shouted Dani and he dropped Fernando and raced over to where he had seen the girl fall. He reached her and knelt down on the ground. He grabbed her head and looked at her face. It was pale in the moonlight but her eyes were still open.

"Dani," she whispered, "did I get him?"

"Yes, you got him all right. Where are you hit?"

"I don't know. I can't feel any pain."

Dani looked her over closely and was relieved to see there were no traces of blood. The bullet must have missed her as she fell over.

"I can't see any wound or anything, here let me help you up." Dani picked her up and she patted herself down a bit just feeling to make sure that she was all intact. The Captain bent and picked up the revolver that she had dropped and slipped it into his jacket pocket.

"How's Fernando?" she asked when she realized that she wasn't hurt.

"He took a bullet in the shoulder, maybe you can take a look at it," suggested Dani trying to keep her mind from thinking about the fact that she had just shot a man. They walked over to Fernando who was sitting where Dani had left him.

"How are you doing friend?" asked the Captain.

"I've been better," admitted the other man. Elizabeth's training kicked in, despite the odd numbness that she was beginning to feel in her brain. She pulled Fernando's hand away from his shoulder so that she could look at his wound. The injured man let out a low groan as she unbuttoned his jacket. As gently as she could she eased it open to get a better look at where the bullet had entered. There was a dark jagged hole through his undershirt and into his flesh and blood was oozing slowly out turning his white undershirt crimson.

Dani looked away, he didn't like seeing his friend in pain. He looked across the glasslike surface of the reservoir to the peaks of the sierras surrounding them. The night air was crisp and clear and if a man had to die then this wouldn't be such a bad place.

"Let's get him back to the ambulance," said Elizabeth, "I've got some dressings in my bag. I need to stem the flow of blood and then I'll be able to make him a bit more comfortable."

Together they helped Fernando back to his feet and then Dani held him sitting upright on the tailgate of the lorry as Elizabeth washed his wound with some water before applying a dressing. Finally she put on the sling they had used to make him appear like a patient at other times during the journey.

"Now you've got a sling for real," she told Fernando who managed to give her a brief smile.

"Here, keep your revolver hidden inside like before," said Dani and he passed the gun to his friend.

"Dani, no, that's going to be uncomfortable for him now," the nurse objected.

"It's all right," said Fernando, "I'll manage. We're a man short now."

Elizabeth's face changed as she remembered who the man was and that she was the one who had shot him.

"Why don't you get some rest in the back *amigo* and Elizabeth can ride up front with me," decided Dani.

They got Fernando settled as comfortably as they could and then went to the cab. Dani started the engine and pulled out onto the road. The first thing he noticed was the bastard petrol gauge with its needle touching empty. Was anything going to go right for them? His only hope was to make it to the next town, but he didn't know how far away that was. Paco must have had a map of some sort in his kitbag, but Dani didn't want to waste any more time by looking for it now. Just how long they had been delayed he wasn't sure, it had seemed like hours, but he knew well enough that time always went more slowly when you were in danger.

"So, what do you think about Fernando's wound," he asked the nurse still trying not to let her have any time to think about what she had done. He knew from his own experience that the first time you killed someone was a terrible occasion.

"We need to get him to a hospital," responded Elizabeth.

"That's not going to be easy I mean there aren't any hospitals up here in the sierras. Hopefully we'll get to Alicante in the morning, we can get a doctor to look at him there."

"He needs to have the bullet removed as soon as possible."

"Yes, I know. As soon as we get there we'll take him to a first aid station."

"I killed a man," wailed Elizabeth all of a sudden and she buried her face in her hands and started to weep. This was all turning into some terrible nightmare from which she knew she would never wake. She felt sure that every time she closed her eyes for the rest of her life she would see Paco's startled face looking at her, frozen in the moment he realized that he had been hit. She wondered what it must feel like to be shot, to know that you were going to die. What would go through your mind? She felt Dani's arm reach around her shoulders to console her and she tried as hard as she could to stop her tears. At the end of the day her tears weren't for Paco, they were for herself.

*

After twenty minutes of hard driving Roberto saw up ahead that the road ran for a while alongside a lake, some sort of mountain reservoir perhaps. It certainly looked beautiful, bathed in the moonlight and framed by the high mountains on the other side.

EIGHTEEN

Dani slowed the lorry to a crawl as they reached the village of Almansa. This was the main pass through the sierras in this area and the village sat in a little hole between the peaks guarded by a castle perched precariously on a steep hill. The castle had a huge tower on one side that made it seem that it was about to topple over and fall down upon the houses below.

If Dani had really hoped to find any petrol here then he was going to be disappointed. The few poor villagers who remained were shut up inside their houses waiting for the war to pass them by, and there probably wasn't a single one who had ever owned a motor vehicle. They had always been farmers looking after small vineyards up on the mountain slopes. They parked the lorry in the little square at the heart of the village where there was a fountain with a slow dribble of water. They filled the radiator and their water bottles and Dani went through Paco's kit bag to try to find the map the driver had been using.

There were two small cans of food, sardines probably and another tin of condensed milk like the one he had shared before. In the end the only plan of the route was a hand drawn map on a small piece of white paper. It showed their journey to Alicante and must have been given to the driver when he took over the lorry in Madrid. It wasn't very detailed at all, but it was all they had. Dani studied it carefully for a minute, noted the fork in the road somewhere up ahead and stuffed it into his diary so that he would know where to find it.

They had no choice but to continue on and hope to get lucky somewhere on the road ahead. As they left Almansa, the lorry's engine began to splutter as it started to feel the lack of fuel. The pass took them between two giant peeks and then came the fork in the road. From Paco's crudely drawn map, Dani knew that they had to take the right hand branch and then it happened, the engine gave a last cough and died. The road was now a gentle downhill slope and so they continued to travel forward for a while until inevitably they came to a standstill as soon as the road tried to climb a little.

"What's up?" Elizabeth wanted to know.

"We've run out of petrol," Dani told her.

116

"What can we do now?" she asked. Dani just gave a shrug and climbed down from the cab to speak to Fernando, maybe he could come up with a miracle solution to their problem.

*

Roberto had his driver go cautiously through the little village of Almansa just in case there was any trouble, but to his relief he found it deserted. They even stopped by the fountain at the central square to have a drink and look up at the strange castle that watched over the place. Everywhere was silent as if there had never been people living there at all.

Once they set off again it wasn't long before they were through the pass and reached the fork in the road. After a quick look at the map they were off again on the right branch that would take them to Alicante.

They hadn't gone far when Roberto saw a dark vehicle parked by the side of the road up ahead. His heart leapt with joy, it could only be one thing.

*

Dani heard the car approaching, its engine splitting the silence of the night. His instinct told him that this was the enemy. They had just been about to have something to eat whilst they delayed having to make a decision about what to do. Dani rushed to the cab and grabbed Paco's rifle. Fernando withdrew his pistol from the sling he was wearing. The Captain motioned for Elizabeth to get into the cab and told her to keep down. He and Fernando then took up a position at the rear of the ambulance on the side away from the road. Dani leant in against the lorry for support and raised his rifle at the oncoming car. When it was within range he squeezed the trigger and a shot rang out.

A bullet smashed through the windscreen and the driver of the car braked hard and veered the vehicle to the right so that they could use it for cover. He and Roberto opened the side doors and tumbled out. It suddenly occurred to them both that they might be outnumbered. Still, time was on their side. If they could prevent the lorry from continuing its journey then help would arrive as soon as the advanced units pushed on from Albacete. How long that would take was anyone's guess, but it did give them some sort of advantage Roberto figured.

Dani's mind was working overtime. There was the very real possibility that more Nationalist forces were on the way. He knew that Albacete had been on the point of surrender when they left and if the fascists had advanced quickly then it was possible that the city had already fallen. He wished he had used the dynamite to blow up the lorry as soon as they had run out of petrol.

Two shots rang out from behind the car as Roberto and the driver fired in the general direction of the lorry, just to let the Reds know that they meant business. Dani raised the rifle to his shoulder once more and looked for a chance to get a shot off, but he couldn't make out a clear target and there was no point in wasting ammunition. He still had the spare bullets that Paco had given him in his jacket pocket, but he definitely didn't have enough to hold off the whole Nationalist advance. Every minute that passed meant that other fascist forces were getting closer. If he hadn't needed the dynamite to blow up the lorry then maybe they could have used it in their present situation.

The suicide option sprang to Dani's mind. If he could somehow get into the back of the lorry then he could use the dynamite and blow them all up along with the ambulance and its special cargo. He pushed that to the back of his mind, there had to be a better plan, besides he didn't want to be responsible for the death of the English nurse. Another two shots rang out breaking the silence, echoing around the mountain peaks.

"Let me try to outflank them," whispered Fernando.

"Okay, I'll cover you," replied Dani. He dropped to one knee held his breath for a second and then quickly leaned forward and fired off a shot. Immediately there came the double reply, one of the bullets so close that Dani could hear it whipping past. Fernando had now left the safety of the lorry and was out in the darkness crouched down low behind a small scrub bush. The pain in his shoulder was unreal, but he gritted his teeth against it and desperately tried to concentrate on not passing out. He waited for Dani to fire again and then he moved off further into the darkness. As soon as he was far enough away not to be seen he would begin to advance.

Roberto realised that there was only one person firing at them. He remembered that one of the pilots he had sent up had seen a nurse and that was why he had fallen for the ambulance ruse, which meant that possibly there was just one soldier and a woman. He liked those odds a lot. He smiled to himself. All they had to do was keep the man wasting his ammunition and then attack him when he ran out.

Dani fired again as quickly as he could. This time one of the bullets that came back flicked through the canvas above him. He wondered how far Fernando had got. He needn't have worried, away in the darkness his friend was moving forward quickly, crouching low and trying not to make any noise. In a few more minutes he would be behind the fascists.

Roberto reloaded his revolver. If there was just one soldier to worry about then his driver could keep him pinned down while Roberto broke cover and made it to the lorry. The nurse must be in the back of the lorry, so if Roberto could get to the front he would be able to slip around to the other side unnoticed and shoot the man from behind. He quickly told his plan to his driver, and when the next shot rang out and Dani ducked back for cover the driver fired off two quick shots and Roberto moved away from the car and began to run along the far side of the road. Before Dani could fire again Roberto's driver fired at the side of the lorry to keep him from looking out. He then fired again as Roberto quickly approached the ambulance.

Fernando was now in a position to be able to see the car clearly in the moonlight. He saw to his horror that there was only one person there. What had happened to the other one? There was no time to lose. Quickly he sprinted forward along the road, his feet crunching in the gravel. The other man suddenly heard him approaching and swung round to see who was coming, but it was too late. Fernando was now close enough to take a shot and he fired just as the crouching man started to raise his gun. The bullet hit the driver in the throat and he instantly dropped his gun and pressed his hands to the place where the bullet had hit him. Fernando watched as a black liquid started to appear between the man's fingers and then he began to cough out blood and collapsed down to the ground with a final choking sound.

Roberto reached the far side of the lorry and began to creep forward. Elizabeth who was hiding in the cab heard his movements. She wanted to warn Dani and Fernando but she couldn't find the voice to scream. She held the hunting knife in her hand and vowed to use it if the man opened the cab door. Fernando started to run back towards the lorry as fast as he could.

Roberto had reached the cab, in a second or two he would be able to sneak around the front.

"Dani, be careful, there's one round behind you," shouted Fernando although he must have known it would draw fire on him. Roberto spun around instantly and fired at the onrushing man. Fernando was hit in the chest. He tried to keep running but he couldn't, it was as if he had run into a wall. He tried to raise his gun to fire but then he felt another bullet kick into him as Roberto fired a second time. Fernando fell to the ground.

Elizabeth heard the man firing from by the cab door and could see the top of his head above the window. Quick as a flash she moved over towards that side, pulled the lever and slammed the door open with all her force. The man was caught by surprise and the impact from the heavy door knocked him to the ground. His gun fell from his grasp as he toppled over. As soon as he hit the gravel, Roberto began scrabbling around to retrieve his weapon. As soon as he had it back in his hand he leapt up towards the open door of the cab.

He was surprised to see a nurse cowering inside. He gave a laugh and raised his pistol to shoot her. A shot rang out and she screamed, but it was Dani who had fired and the shot hit Roberto in the side and swung him around. As Roberto came to face him Dani fired again, this time hitting him in the heart. The Nationalist Captain's face turned from disbelief into a strange determined grimace and although his gun had fallen to the floor he took a step towards Dani as if he meant to strangle him with his bare hands. Dani fired again and this time the man fell backwards clutching at the side of the lorry to try to stop himself from falling, but he couldn't get a grip of anything and he went down to the ground in an untidy heap.

Dani went to the cab and peered in. He saw Elizabeth there, her eyes strangely glazed over, a hunting knife in her hands ready to kill.

"It's okay Beth, it's me," he said soothingly. He saw her face relax as she looked into his eyes and then she moved across the cab and jumped down into his arms. He held her tight as they both began to come to terms with the fact that they were still alive. Then Dani remembered Fernando. He let go of the nurse and ran over to where his friend lay in the road. He knelt down beside him and cradled his friend's head in his hands. Fernando's face looked ghastly in the moonlight here on this godforsaken road and Dani swallowed hard as tears started to well up behind his eyes. Elizabeth came over and crouched down beside the Captain and embraced him as he cried for his dear friend. She cried too and this time the tears were not for herself.

NINETEEN

After a while Dani wiped the last tears from his eyes and stood up to look at Elizabeth. He was glad that he wasn't alone because if he had been then he would probably have just sat down there in the road beside his dead friend and waited for the Rebel advance to come and get him. As it was, the presence of the girl meant that he was still responsible for someone, and that meant he had to carry on, even if he didn't want to.

"We ought to blow up the lorry," said the Captain wiping his sleeve across his eyes and looking at Elizabeth's pale and frightened face.

"We can use their car," she whispered touching his face with trembling fingers. "We can put the crates into the back of the car. We can still do this Dani, we owe it to Fernando who gave his life for this mission." Dani knew that Fernando had not given his life for the mission, he had simply given it for a friend, but she was right, they couldn't just give up now. They had a car with petrol although how much it had in the tank he didn't know and whilst they probably couldn't fit all the crates into the car without breaking its axels, they could certainly manage to take some of the load. He knew it would take hours to transfer the heavy crates and that the fascists could be upon them at any moment, but the girl was right, they had to try. They could just blow up the lorry and save themselves and drive to Valencia or Cartagena and hope to get on a ship to safety, but Fernando would never have been happy with that.

"I want to bury my friend first," decided the Captain.

"Sure," whispered Elizabeth although she knew it would take a lot of time. Dani walked over to the car to see if they had a spade in the boot by any chance. They might do since they would have made any prisoners dig their own graves before shooting them. He took the key from the ignition and cautiously opened the car's tiny boot. There was no spade inside, just a couple of small fuel cans. Dani felt his heart jump for joy, but stopped himself when he thought that they were probably empty. Nevertheless, with a shaking hand he pulled one of them out of the boot. It was full. He set it down on the ground and then tried the other one. It was also full. He shouted with delight and Elizabeth came running over to see what he had found.

"Petrol," he said holding up the can in his hand.

122

"Oh my god!" exclaimed the nurse.

Dani emptied the two small cans of fuel into the lorry's tank and hoped that it would be enough to get them to Alicante. Then he lifted his friend's lifeless body up under the armpits and half dragged half carried it off the road and into the rough scrubland. They had no means of digging a grave in the hard earth, but Dani scraped out a small hollow using his boot and then he and Elizabeth piled rocks around and then on top of the body. It would keep it safe from wild animals for a while at least. When they had finished, they stood together heads bowed looking at the makeshift grave. The nurse thought that Dani might say a prayer, but of course religion had faded away in the Republican zone.

"Go with god *amigo*," he said and then he made the clenched fist salute as he and Fernando had made together at many makeshift gravesides throughout the long months of war. "Viva la República," he finally shouted so that it rebounded off the mountains. Dani swore to himself that one day he would return and mark his friend's final resting place with some sort of memorial. They placed Fernando's cap on a stick and drove it into the pile of rocks and then they went back to the ambulance.

They set off along the road once more, in silence. Elizabeth wanted to say something to Dani to try to comfort him but all the words that came into her head seemed insufficient and so she said nothing. Instead, after a while, she found herself wondering what would happen when they reached Alicante. Would she be put on a ship to Mexico or worse still to Russia? Would Dani be able to go with her? Surely if he succeeded in this near impossible mission the least he deserved was the chance to escape. He had risked his life for the cause and surely the cause wasn't now just going to abandon him? And if they did escape, what then? Could she just go back to her parents' house in Bournemouth and return to normal? And Dani? Where would he go? He wouldn't be able to return to his home in Spain that was for sure. Although he spoke fluent English he had never lived in England, it would be difficult for him to settle there alone. And it would be even worse if he had to stay in Mexico or, god forbid, Russia. The thought of being separated from him for the rest of her life suddenly filled her with a profound sorrow.

At last they were into the region of Alicante. The first place they came to was Villena and here they were stopped at a makeshift roadblock at the entrance to the town. There were only a couple of elderly men on guard who said they belonged to the local communist militia. Elizabeth told them in her wavering Spanish that they had had a fight with some fascists and that the enemy would be with them in no time at all. She begged them not to delay them as they had to get to Alicante urgently. She flashed them her most beautiful smile and no doubt reminded them of their daughters and so they stood aside for the ambulance to pass through.

"Save yourselves," Dani shouted to the men as he drove the lorry through the barricade and into the town. As they had seen in most of the places they had passed through the town was deserted and ghostly. The little main street lined with tall naked trees was flanked by double-storey houses that had seen better days. Here the war had left it late to arrive, but arrive it would and in its most confusing form. They just caught a glimpse of another stunning castle, perhaps the most beautiful of their journey so far had they really been looking at them, and then they were out of the town and crossing the river just as it began to grow light.

*

The General woke up as the first rays of light began to filter through the gaps in the shutters. Today was the day, his last in Spain, and not a day too soon. News was in from Albacete that the enemy had arrived during the late evening and that the city would surrender at dawn. From there the Rebel advance would push on towards the coast and it wouldn't take long to arrive. The streets of Alicante were packed with people hoping that there would be some sort of organised evacuation, but the General knew there wouldn't be. The only ship remaining in the harbour was his and that would sail at midday bound for Mexico, and only a very few high-ranking Republican officials would be able to afford the price of safety.

The General had given orders that if his lorry arrived in the night then he was to be woken, whatever time it was. But since no one had come it meant that the ambulance still hadn't got there. He wondered if he had made a mistake putting that young *malageño* captain in charge, but then there hadn't been too many alternatives. He had delayed his departure from Madrid to the last possible moment to set up the transfer of his goods, and he had almost delayed too much. He had taken off from

Cuatro Vientos just as the Rebels were entering the city and flown to Albacete. The whole journey he had been on edge in case they were spotted by enemy fighters, and when they had touched down at Los Llanos he had been a very relieved man. To find a car waiting for him had also been a huge relief. So far everything in his neatly contrived plan had gone smoothly, everything except the arrival of the damn lorry.

If it didn't arrive by midday then the ship would sail without it. He wondered what could have happened to it. There were so many possibilities for failure that it depressed him to think about them. The ambulance could have been attacked by enemy planes, or overtaken by the fascist advance. Maybe those he had trusted had opened the crates against his specific orders and decided to steal his cargo. It was possible that the lorry might have broken down somewhere on route although he had found a new American vehicle for them in the hope that it would be more reliable, or perhaps they had run out of fuel. He had ordered plenty of spare cans to be stored on board the lorry, but petrol in Madrid was so scarce that anyone involved might have stolen a can to sell for a small fortune on the black market. He knew he hadn't been the only high-ranking officer looking to flee south, and not all of them would have had his bargaining power with the air force, many were desperately trying to get hold of petrol for their staff cars. Could it be that the lorry he was waiting for was parked at some desolate roadside with no more fuel? He hoped then that Dani would blow it up rather than let it fall into fascist hands, and of course blow himself up too, and the others with him, although it would be a shame about the English nurse. He had heard from his adjutant that she was very pretty. Perhaps he could take her along on his trip to Mexico, yes, that would do nicely, his personal nurse for the whole voyage. If she refused to cater to his every whim then he would just have her thrown overboard.

The General somehow managed to haul his ungainly bulk out of the bed. He was glad that he wouldn't have to spend another night in its sweaty clutches. There was a large porcelain bowl of water and he washed his jowled face and then put on his best uniform that had been neatly pressed the night before. He was ready for breakfast. He had told his adjutant that he wanted *churros* for his last meal on Spanish soil although it was difficult to imagine that there was anywhere in Alicante at that time that might have the wherewithal to produce them. Anyway, it didn't really matter. Soon he would be eating Mexican food at some beach paradise surrounded by his live-in voluptuous *mejicana* maids. All this if only that lorry would arrive in time.

*

Dani stopped just past the village of Petrer and he and Elizabeth got out to stretch their legs. They breakfasted on condensed milk and the bread that the nurse had saved from Albacete. It was so hard and stale that they had to open the can of condensed milk up completely and dip small pieces of the bread into it to make them chewable. Still, Dani wasn't complaining, he had known many mornings when there had been nothing at all for breakfast despite the great foraging skills of his friend Fernando. He was glad that he wouldn't have to go back to Malaga and face his friend's family, especially his four sisters who had all loved him with exaggeration. They had all been killed in the bombing the same as Dani's parents. He wondered if he would ever get back to his place of birth or would Alicante be as close as he ever came?

They didn't stop for long, the sun was beginning to climb and that meant that enemy planes might be up looking for targets, besides, it had been a long nerve-wracking journey and Dani wanted it to come to an end as soon as possible. They were now in El Cid country travelling through the final sierras on the way down to the coast. They would pass close to Elche where the famous Cid had lived in the winter of 1088 and enter the city of Alicante from the south not too far from the port.

They travelled these last few kilometres in near silence, both worried about what kind of reception they might receive when they reached their destination. So far, all of Dani's attention had been focussed on getting to Alicante nothing else had been important, but now he realised that he would have to think about saving himself from the fascists. It wouldn't be easy. He doubted very much that the General would find a place for him on a ship, why would he? Dani was only a Captain, there must be far more important people clamouring to get away. He would do his best to see that Elizabeth was guaranteed a safe way out of the war. Maybe the British would have a boat there to take away any of their citizens who were trapped on the coast, although there can't have been many who had not already left.

As they approached the city so the road became choked with refugees. Dani slowed the lorry to a crawl and resigned himself to the fact that they wouldn't get there quite as quickly as he had hoped. Every Republican who feared reprisals would be heading if not for Alicante then for Valencia or Cartagena the other two Mediterranean Republican ports. The big question that everyone wanted answering was would there be ships there to take them to safety?

TWENTY

At last they saw Alicante's castle perched up high on the towering hill that dominated the city. In a bygone age any enemy seeing it for the first time would have thought it impossible to take this seaport, but times and wars had changed and castles no longer defended cities like this. As they drove through the suburbs they could see the scars of the bombardments that had taken place throughout the war, some houses were half blown away and the road snaked slowly around bomb craters. Dani glanced at the petrol gauge, not that it mattered now, and saw that the tank was nearly empty, they had just made it.

The target of the bombing raids of course had been the harbour and the docks, but the civilian population had suffered too at the hands of the squadrons of Italian and German planes. There had been repeated attacks whenever the Republican fleet had been in port and now, when the people needed the fleet, it was too dangerous for any Republican captain to even consider approaching. The Rebels had total domination of the skies and most of the antiaircraft batteries around the docks were no longer in fighting order. The only ships that might consider entering were from neutral countries, like Mexico, but even they were taking a huge risk.

*

The General was pacing back and forth along the loading area in the docks waiting for news of the lorry and worried that time was running out. If the ship was to catch the tide at midday then everything would have to be loaded well before hand. In fact the ship was almost completely ready, the only space being that left for the General's cargo. It had been decided that it would be easier simply to winch the whole lorry into the ship's hold rather than unload the containers and put them in one by one. A huge crane was waiting nearby to pick up the lorry as soon as it arrived.

With an hour to go before sailing, dark smoke began to plume out of the ship's funnel as the stokers began to fire up the burners, and the General was forced to concede that he would have to set sail for Mexico alone. He went to look for his adjutant to tell him to take his bags on board.

He found his adjutant talking excitedly on the phone with the soldiers who were acting as port security, basically keeping out anyone except the most high-ranking Republican officials and their families.

"Your lorry is at the gate comrade General," gushed the man.

"Really? I don't believe it," gasped the General. "Tell them to let it through without delay and tell them they should drive around to the back of the warehouse for immediate loading."

The adjutant relayed instructions and then the General told him that they would go to the back of the warehouse to meet up with the lorry and inspect its precious cargo.

Dani was amazed that his orders had been accepted and that after a brief phone call they were being allowed through. He had driven the lorry through masses of people who had all been refused entry to the docks. One of the soldiers raised the barrier and waved them inside. The Captain had been told to drive around to the back of a warehouse where the General would be waiting for them.

As they rounded the corner of the huge building they saw the podgy General striding towards them in an excited manner, his face beaming like a child about to receive his birthday presents. Dani brought the lorry to a standstill and opened his window.

"Good morning comrade Captain," laughed the General, "I was beginning to think that you weren't going to make it."

"There were times when I thought we wouldn't make it comrade General," replied Dani.

"Yes I'm sure," said the General dismissively. "If you pull the lorry into the warehouse we can have a quick look at the cargo, make sure it's all there and then get it loaded, the ship sails at midday."

"We just made it then," said Dani relieved that he hadn't decided to park up for the day. He was beginning to feel a real sense of euphoria spreading through his brain. He couldn't begin to believe that they had made it all this way against all the odds. He was proud to have been of service to the Republic one last time. He stopped the lorry in the huge empty warehouse and he and the nurse climbed down from the cab. The only thing left on Dani's mind was Elizabeth's safety.

"Listen, comrade General, can you tell me what's going to happen to the English nurse?"

"The nurse? Yes, I was thinking that it would be useful to have a nurse along for the trip to Mexico."

"So she'll be safe?"

"Quite safe. When we get to Mexico I'll see about getting her back to England."

"And what about the Captain, comrade General?" asked Elizabeth who had been following the conversation. The General put an arm around her waist and pulled her close to him. Suddenly the General switched into English which surprised everyone.

"The Captain is going to be shot my dear, so don't worry yourself about him. Yes, I speak English, I was at Oxford when I was younger." The General who had only known Dani as Captain Gonzalez had no idea that the other man had understood what he had said. Quickly Dani's hand went to his revolver, but the General's adjutant was quicker and had his own weapon at the Captain's temple. If Elizabeth hadn't been there Dani would have shot the General anyway and let the other man kill him, but there was every chance that he would then shoot the nurse too. The adjutant held out his hand and Dani reluctantly handed over his weapon.

"Take him outside and shoot him," ordered the General. "I don't want it done in front of the *señorita*. Throw his body into the water."

"Yes, comrade General," responded the adjutant with a smile.

"Come now then my pretty nurse," continued the General, "why don't you come and take a look at my gold."

"Gold?" questioned Elizabeth not sure that she had heard him correctly.

"There's gold in those crates?" asked Dani.

"Of course, of course," laughed the General. "My gold."

"You mean the Republic's gold, don't you?" said Dani.

"Let's just look at it as my retirement payment from the Republic, shall we?"

"You mean you're stealing it?"

"The Republic has ceased to exist young man, it's everyone for himself now."

"So my friend Fernando died so that you could enjoy a long and happy exile in Mexico?"

"Did someone die? I'm sorry about that. Now take him outside and shoot him," snapped the General losing patience.

130

The adjutant grabbed Dani by the arm and started to lead him over to the huge warehouse doors through which he had driven the ambulance.

"Wait," shouted Elizabeth, "please don't shoot him. You've got your gold and it's all thanks to that man, how can you repay him like this?"

"Life's not fair," stated the General philosophically. Elizabeth tried to think quickly of something she could do to save Dani.

"Listen comrade General, would you at least let me give the comrade Captain a goodbye hug. He saved my life and I'd like to say *adiós*. Of course, if you grant me this tiny favour, well maybe I'll be able to do a little favour for you in return," she said licking her lips. The General got the message. This was exactly what he had been hoping for, a beautiful foreign woman to keep him company on the long voyage ahead.

"Okay," he decided. "A quick *abrazo* and then the Captain gets shot."

Elizabeth walked over to Dani, one hand touching the knife hidden in the waistband of her skirt. The adjutant stepped back to give them some room and the Nurse embraced the Captain to her with one arm, shielding her other side from the adjutant. Quickly she slipped the knife into Dani's hand. He knew what it was straight away and managed to push it inside his jacket.

"That's enough," barked the General. The two young people separated and Dani allowed himself to be taken outside. As soon as they were out of the doors he twisted the adjutant around, pressing him back against the wall forcing the hand with the gun upwards and thrusting the knife up into his chest. The man looked startled and Dani clamped a hand over his mouth before he could cry out. The Captain twisted the knife harder still up under the adjutant's rib cage. Dani then pushed him down to the ground and took the man's gun. The General was expecting to hear a gunshot so the Captain fired at the other man in the head. He then dumped the body off the side of the docks into the oily murk of the harbour.

Inside the warehouse, the General was waiting impatiently for his adjutant to return so that he could inspect his gold. It had been hidden away for so long and he hadn't had a chance to look at it before it was loaded and he was impatient to see its beautiful sparkle. His adjutant had the key to the padlocks and when he came back they could open the containers together. He was sure that the nurse would be impressed when she saw the gold, his gold. No doubt the promise of a small share when they reached Mexico might help to keep her agreeable during the voyage.

Impatient to see his precious gold, the General walked round to the back of the ambulance and started to try to haul himself up. He heard footsteps approaching and assumed it was his adjutant.

"Give me a hand up will you," he called. "Maybe when I've finished with her I'll let you have a go with that nurse, what do you say to that?"

"I don't think so General," said Dani.

The fat General stopped half way up the back of the lorry and turned in horror to see the young Captain he had ordered to be killed standing before him.

"But how?" stammered the General.

"We've been through hell to get this lorry here from Madrid and now you tell us that it's full of gold that you're stealing from the Republic, I'm sorry but that just isn't going to happen."

"Shoot him Dani," urged Elizabeth who was standing by his side.

"Listen, hold on a bit. Let's just think about this for a second shall we. There's a lot of gold in this lorry," said the General climbing back down from the ambulance. "I'm willing to pay you a large sum of money to let me live, a very large sum of money. I'll also pay your passage on the boat. Think about what your life would be like as a rich man in Mexico."

"This gold isn't yours to barter with," Dani told him, "it belongs to the Spanish Republic and I'm going to see that it doesn't fall into enemy hands."

"Shoot him Dani," whispered Elizabeth again. The Captain raised the gun and looked at the General standing before him. The General sank slowly to his knees and bowed his head, there was the sound of quiet sobbing. Dani thought about his friend Fernando, about Paco the driver and about all the others who had died for the General's gold, but he wasn't a murderer. He just couldn't shoot a man in cold blood whoever he was and whatever he had done.

"Come on Beth, we should leave. Another death won't do any good."

"You're going to let him escape?"

"I don't think he'll get too far without his gold, when the people who were going to help him realise that he can't pay for their services he'll be just another ex-Republican General waiting for execution."

Reluctantly Elizabeth followed Dani back to the cab and climbed in. They left the General kneeling on the floor in the middle of the huge empty warehouse and went back towards the barriers through which they had passed earlier. Hearing them approaching the guards turned in disbelief, surely no one would want to drive away from the docks at this time with the last ship about to leave.

"Comrade Captain?" said the man suspicion written all over his face as he leaned into Dani's window.

"We've been told to go to Cartagena," Dani informed him.

"Orders?"

Dani made as if to reach into his jacket and at the same time pushed his foot down hard on the accelerator and the lorry crashed through the barrier and out of the restricted area. The soldier was thrown to the floor, but his companion who had been chatting to a pretty girl who was desperately trying to use her charms to get into the docks, raised his rifle and fired at the ambulance. Screaming and shouting followed from the masses of refugees who had been waiting there and then there was a stampede as people saw the barrier was broken and the soldiers distracted. Thousands of desperate people surged through into the previously restricted area and headed for the waterfront and some imagined salvation.

Dani threaded the lorry back out of the port area carefully avoiding the masses of people who were going in the opposite direction. As soon as they were clear of the docks he headed south to pick up the coast road that would take them past the airbase at El Altet and on towards Cartagena. They had no hope of ever reaching there, not without any fuel, but no hope had become a way of life for Dani over the last few months. He figured that the Rebels would take Valencia and Alicante first and worry about Cartagena later, maybe those extra hours might help save them.

TWENTY-ONE

February 2009

It was raining. It was always raining lately or was that just that I was always in a foul mood lately? In fact, there were flecks of snow in the air as I hurried from London Bridge station to the office. It was the beginning of February, but even so, didn't I, like every bewildered commuter, already long for spring? These were the worst months of the year. Christmas was long gone (for those who like Christmas) and the changing of the clocks that would herald the arrival of better days still seemed a lifetime away. There was nothing to look forward to, just the misery of short cold days with a dark ceiling of low grey cloud for weeks on end. These were days when the sun never appeared. Days when the only daylight I saw was during this five minute furtive scurry from train station to office in the morning. When I left home to walk to the station it was still dark and by the end of the working day it was of course already dark again. Had I thought to take my lunch hour I could have gone for a freezing walk by the river or a quick flit to the shops, but lunch hour was a luxury I didn't bother with in the winter. I just stayed at my desk with a sandwich and a can of coke from a vending machine and worked my arse off. It was for the best. It was work that had kept me sane after the disintegration of my marriage and I was grateful to be doing something.

In the spring, I might think about getting my life back into some sort of order, but for now I just wanted to keep myself to myself, my tail between my legs and lick my wounds in private. The rest of the translators in my office realised that I needed to be left alone and kept conversations to a minimum, never straying far from the mundane. They used me to check over stuff they were having difficulties with and which was taking up too much of their time, or passed me the extra boring crap that no one else had the heart to tackle. I did it all, and I was even grateful for it. The boss had reminded me recently that I hadn't taken any holiday for a long time and that if I didn't take some soon I might start to lose it. I had worked all through the summer and all over Christmas, and my intention was to work all through the rest of the winter and wait for the spring. Maybe when the spring came I wouldn't be able to face it and I would just work on through to the summer again.

134

I knew that days off work would be just like the weekends, hours of misery cooped up in my tiny flat with just the TV for company. My only friend was alcohol, and even alcohol wasn't helping much.

It's amazing how much your life can change in just a short space of time. For example, the ten seconds or so it took my wife to say "I'm leaving you," turned my world upside down in an instant. It's true we hadn't been happy for a long time, maybe years, but I always hoped that things might change for the better. I thought perhaps we might somehow come across a way to get back what we had lost. We hadn't even argued much, we just sort of kept ourselves to ourselves. Unknowingly, we had divided our house into his and hers areas, even the bed had come to have an invisible line down the middle over which neither bothered to stray.

I hadn't realised she had been cheating on me, perhaps I hadn't wanted to, I don't know. So it came as a genuine shock when she announced that she was leaving me for some guy at her work. No doubt they had more in common. They certainly saw more of each other. It was lucky that we had never had children I guess, it would have made the situation even harder to bear. We always reckoned that one day we would have a child, but the years slipped by and we never took the decision, fear of the unknown maybe or a lack of real interest perhaps. I think once I got over the initial shock at being left I wasn't sad, I just felt sorry for myself that's all. I vowed to get my life back on line and make the most of this unexpected second chance to find happiness, but happiness was proving more elusive now than it had been before. I kept telling myself that come the spring I would make a big effort to find myself a new life, but I wasn't sure if I was just kidding myself or not.

I packed my most personal possessions into cardboard boxes and moved into a little rented flat in another town a few stops farther away from London where I knew no one and no one knew me. At least I got a seat on the train in the mornings now, although my journey was fifteen minutes longer each way. My wife decided to buy out my share of our little terraced house and move in with her new man who had left his wife and three kids to be with her (the idiot). So I had a sum of money in the bank to use as a deposit to buy a place in the spring, but for now I just rented.

I reached the office half an hour earlier than everyone else, as usual, and let myself in. Coffee was the first order of the day, and still with my coat on I went into the little kitchen and filled the kettle. I then moved around our office space turning on lights until I got to my desk over against the far wall. I switched on my computer and finally took off my coat hanging it on the coat rack beside the umbrella stand. A lot of people hate their place of work, but I didn't, I just sort of accepted it. The same with the people I worked with, I just accepted them. They weren't friends and they weren't enemies. I didn't even mind the boss. It was her who kept me loaded down with worthless tasks and I was grateful to her for that.

This morning I was glad to have a particularly nasty piece to work on, I'd given it a quick glance over the previous evening when it had arrived and it looked like a monster. A translation of a booklet about how to use some state of the art Mexican drilling head for offshore oil exploration, and of course it was urgent. I studied my shelf of trusty dictionaries and reference books and took down three which I thought might be useful and placed them on my desk then I went back to the kitchen to get myself a coffee.

I was just adding the milk and sugar when the office door opened and the boss came in shaking her umbrella.

"God, it's cold today," she announced.

"Cup of tea?" I offered.

"Thanks," she replied heading to the door of her little office. So I put off my Mexican drill bit text for a few minutes more, but I knew it would get done by the end of the morning. I took the steaming cup of coffee to my boss' office and placed it on the coaster by her computer screen. She was trying to get the worst of the tangles out of her hair after hanging up her coat on the back of the door. I saw that her computer screen was showing signs of life. She would quickly check on the new jobs that had been sent in and allocate them to whoever she thought most suitable before the others arrived. I knew she didn't want to be disturbed at that time and I left her to it. We'd worked together for so long. She'd started there a year after me, but when the old boss was moved to our office in Geneva, she was the one that got the promotion, not me. I wasn't mad or anything, just disappointed with myself for not being good enough I guess. We'd never talked about it and probably never would. She was an expert in

French and that made up the bulk of the company's work whilst I handled the lesser flow of Spanish stuff. There were people with other languages too, of course, and there were those really bright bastards who moved between languages like clever ghosts, a bit of German, some French, lunch and then a couple of hours wrestling with something Italian. I didn't really envy them their variety, I was happy with my Spanish. It was the only thing I had ever been good at.

So here I was, thirty-nine and fucked. Soon I would be fucked at forty, the thought of which would have sent me into a depression had I not already been there. But anyway, depressed or not I was still hanging in there at work, still pulling out all the stops when it came to scientific reports, complicated instruction manuals, the occasional novel or history book and of course texts about Mexican off-shore drill bits.

I was just closing in on the final paragraph of my text and thinking about a trip to the vending machine for lunch when the phone on my desk rang and scared the life out of me. Some of the younger people I worked with seemed to be on the phone all the time, mainly social calls from friends about where to meet up for lunch or where they should go after work for a few cocktails, but my phone hardly ever rang.

I picked it up suspiciously, thinking that one of the younger crowd had routed a call to my extension by mistake. It was the secretary who handled all the incoming calls who had a desk in the other office with a view of the street.

"Hi Daniel, there's a call for you," she said quickly and efficiently and I heard a click as my caller was put through.

"Hello?" I asked.

"Hello there," said a female Scottish voice. "Is that Daniel Miller?"

"Yes, it is."

"Listen, I'm calling from the Royal Infirmary in Edinburgh, I'm sorry to have to tell you that your father has suffered a severe heart attack and is here at the hospital."

"What?" it was all I could think of off the top of my head.

"Yes," continued the voice patiently no doubt used to having to impart unbelievable news, "your father suffered a heart attack this morning and we've just managed to track you down as his next of kin with the help of the police."

"So, how is he?" I managed although that wasn't the first question that came to mind. The first was what the fuck is he doing in Edinburgh?

"He's in a coma at the moment. I'm afraid the doctor's prognosis isn't too optimistic at this stage. Maybe you ought to think about coming for a talk with the doctor yourself."

"To Edinburgh?"

"Yes. I'm afraid so, Edinburgh."

"Which hospital did you say again?" I asked fumbling for a pen and paper.

"The Royal Infirmary of Edinburgh."

"And which ward is he on?"

"He's still in A&E at the moment, we're waiting for a bed in Intensive Care."

"I see, Intensive Care. So, it's quite serious then."

"Yes, Mr Miller, it's quite serious. He's in a coma, he's rather poorly I'm afraid."

"Okay, I'll get there as soon as I can. Obviously it's going to take me a while, I'm here in London."

"I know Mr Miller. Just get here as quickly as you can. Sorry to have to give you such bad news."

"Thank you," I said.

"Bye now," said the Scottish voice and she was gone. After I put the phone down, I just sat there numb while a million thoughts raced through my mind. Good god, my father was alive, well, in a coma, but still he was alive. In Edinburgh. After all these years of wondering was he dead or alive and now he turns up in a coma in Edinburgh. What the hell was he doing in Edinburgh? How the hell had the police there managed to track me down at work? The phone rang again. This couldn't be happening could it? Not two phone calls in the same day? I was going to get phone-flustered.

"Hi Daniel, there's another call for you. She says she's your ex-wife." The secretary was new and probably didn't know too much about my personal life or more than likely she just wasn't interested enough to have asked anyone about me. The phone clicked as my caller was put through, no way out now.

"Hi, Daniel, Danny, it's me."

138

"Hello." It was the first time I had heard her voice since we went to court to get divorced, everything since, mainly the purchase of my half of the house (minus the remaining mortgage and costs) had been by letter via our solicitors.

"I just got a phone call from the police in Edinburgh." So that explains how the hospital found me at work, although it didn't explain what my ex was doing at home during the day.

"Yes, my father's had a heart attack, he's in a hospital in Edinburgh."

"Your father? Really? In Edinburgh?"

"Yes."

"I thought you hadn't heard from your father since you were a kid?"

"I haven't."

"Oh. Is he okay?"

"No, not really, he's in a coma and they're waiting for a bed in Intensive Care."

"I'm sorry about that."

"It's all right."

"What are you going to do?"

"I guess I'd better go up to Edinburgh, I haven't had time to think about it yet, I just got the call a minute ago."

"You can borrow the car if you want." That would be my car she had insisted on keeping for a few weeks when we split up as she travelled about a bit for work and had never returned to me. Still, I hadn't asked for it back and I wouldn't have used it anyway, I didn't go anywhere.

"It's okay. I think I'll fly, it'll be the quickest way to get there."

"I thought you hated flying?" Shit, busted. In the last few years of our marriage I'd made up a fear of flying in order to get out of going on holiday with her for any length of time.

"What were you doing at home during the day?" I asked changing the subject as quickly as I could.

"I'm on pregnancy leave," she replied. Fuck me. Now she was ramming home the fact that she was having sex with another man.

"I didn't think you wanted kids," I said.

"It was you who didn't want kids, anyway, let's not get into that now, there's no point to it." She was right of course.

"When's it due?" I asked.

"Any day now."

"Well, good luck with that. I hope everything goes smoothly."

"Thank you. And I hope your father's all right."

"Thanks. Well, I'd better go, got a flight to book."

"Okay then, bye."

"Goodbye." At last I could put the phone down on her. Pregnant hey? Well, fuck me, did I already say that?

Okay, think. Tell the boss or check on the flight situation, which should I do first? Finish the Mexican text I decided. There was no point in leaving it with just one paragraph to go. I didn't know how long I would be away from my desk and of course it was urgent. Ten minutes later it was finished and I sent it off. Someone somewhere could now get on with using their new Mexican drill bit in total safety, I was sure they couldn't wait.

I decided that the next step was to talk to the boss. I couldn't imagine her saying that I couldn't leave, it was a genuine emergency after all, and besides I was not one of those people who was always begging for time off. I hadn't taken a sick day in years either. But, it was best to check with her first.

Her office door was open, it usually was and I knocked quietly to inform her of my presence. She turned away from her computer screen towards me.

"What's up?" she asked stifling a yawn with the back of her hand and flexing her neck muscles slightly.

"I wondered if I could have a word."

"Sure, go ahead."

"No, in private," I said.

"Oh, sure. Shut the door then." I shut the door.

TWENTY-TWO

When I left the boss' office I went back to my desk to use the internet to look for a flight. It was just after one when I finished talking to the boss. I checked the British Airways website and settled on a flight leaving Heathrow at 16.15 which gave me plenty of time to get to the airport and check in. Shit, I would have nothing to check in. I didn't even have a change of clothes or a toothbrush. A quick shopping spree was called for I decided, but first I had to book myself into a hotel for a couple of nights.

*

The flight landed on time and I was soon on the bus into Edinburgh. I had never been to Scotland before, hell the farthest north I had ever been was probably Camden Town. My journey now was for all the wrong reasons but I was excited nevertheless to be going somewhere so unknown. This was the first solo adventure I had had for as long as I could remember and I was more nervous than I had been since I went off to live in Spain when I was at the university in Salamanca for a year. Then I had been just a kid on a spectacular adventure, now I was a self-doubting middle-aged fool going to see his estranged dying father.

The bus dropped me next to the station and I walked for about ten minutes to find my little hotel, my printed internet map guiding me there. It was tucked away in a leafy side street and I was soon checked in. I asked the receptionist how to get to the Royal Infirmary and she told me where I could catch a bus and which number would get me there.

Walking into the hospital it suddenly struck me that I didn't have a clue what my father looked like. And what would be his reaction if he awoke from his coma to find some strange bloke sitting at his bedside? And then of course there was the possibility that I was already too late, that he had died during my long journey north. I took a deep breath and approached the main reception desk. After a quick check on the computer I was off down a long corridor towards Intensive Care.

A young nurse led me to my father's room and I found a strange man with an untidy grey/black beard hooked up to one of those breathing machines, the hissing sound it made every second or so making it seem that each breath would be his last. The nurse told me she would try to get the doctor to come and talk to me and disappeared leaving me alone with this man I couldn't even remember. I stood and stared at his face, pale as death apart from the unkempt beard and tried to think of something to say.

But what could I say? What could you say to someone who had left your mother to fend for herself when you were three years old? To someone who had never sent a penny to buy you a bike or a pair of football boots? To someone who hadn't even sent a card for your birthday?

"Mum's dead," I said. "I don't know if you can hear me or anything, but mum's dead. She died last year, breast cancer, thought you ought to know."

I sat down and waited for the doctor.

*

It turned into a long wait, a couple of hours at least and then the doctor breezed in all matter-of-factly and told me that my father's situation was hopeless and that it was only machines that were keeping him alive. I should think about when they ought to turn off life support and let him pass away and perhaps I could give a bit of thought to whether or not my father would have wished to donate some of his organs to help save others. He left.

"Your father's personal possessions are in the cupboard over there," said the nurse quietly. "He had a heart attack in the street and the ambulance brought him straight here, there's just his clothes, a wallet and his house keys, that's all."

I went over to the cupboard and looked at his things, and just as the nurse had said there was a neatly folded stack of shabby clothes next to a black leather wallet with a set of keys on top. I picked up the wallet and opened it. There were a couple of ten pound notes a library card and some old receipts. There was no driver's licence and no credit cards. I looked at the library card and found it had an address on it so I now knew where he lived. I wondered if he lived alone or if there was someone in his life. The fact that I was the only one who had come to the hospital indicated that he was probably alone. I began to feel a bit sorry for him. On further examination of the wallet I discovered a small square photograph in the lining. I tugged it out and saw the face of a baby

142

looking back at me, a baby that couldn't be more than five or six months old. I turned the picture over and found 'Daniel September 1970' written on the back. My heart seemed to stop all of a sudden and I had to gasp for breath. This man had kept my photograph in his wallet for the best part of forty years. He had carried it with him everywhere. I sat down. I slipped the wallet and keys into my jacket pocket for safe keeping.

I looked at his face again and it didn't seem so alien now. He was resting peacefully and it seemed that at any moment he might wake up and I might be able to talk to him. I wanted to ask him why he had left us all those years ago and why he had never bothered to keep in touch, but they were questions to which I would never get answers. My mother had always said he just left one day and that was all she would say.

The nurse returned and said that it was nearly eleven and that I should think about going to get some rest after my long journey and then come back in the morning. I would need a clear head in order to make some important decisions. I gave her my mobile number and she promised to ring if there was any change in his condition although she was pretty sure there wouldn't be.

Outside I was hit by a stab of cold after the barmy heat of the hospital and I realised that my London coat wasn't up to the job here in the Scottish capital. I stood at the bus stop for a long while, stamping my feet and blowing on my hands until at last a bus arrived, empty but for an old woman sitting behind the driver.

*

The next morning I was up early and sat down to a good breakfast. I hadn't eaten anything the previous evening and my stomach had been rumbling all night, so as soon as it had sensed the beginning of breakfast preparations at around seven thirty it had me up and showered and sitting in the dining room.

I got the receptionist to call me a cab and it took me to the address on the library card from my father's wallet. I wanted to see where he had been living and also just check that there was no one who might be missing him. If he had lived with someone then they might be able to help me with the decision of when to let my father pass away. They might also be able to tell me something about this man I had always wanted to get to know.

It was a small terraced house in the outskirts with a door that opened directly onto the street. It was in need of a lick of paint around the windows and the bare bricks were dirty, but it didn't seem too bad. I rang the doorbell a couple of times and then nervously tried the key in the lock. It opened and I shouted a greeting to anyone who might be there, there was no reply. I went in and shut the door. My heart was pounding a hundred times faster than normal and I felt like a burglar standing in a stranger's house I had no right to be in.

There was a little front room, a few discarded newspapers thrown across an old sofa and a TV on a low sideboard, an empty pizza box and a couple of empty cans of bitter on the coffee table. From there I went into the kitchen which was a cramped, dark place with dirty-brown cupboards. There was a back door to a small overgrown garden. I went back to the hallway and climbed the stairs. At the top of the stairs there was a bathroom and then my father's bedroom. The bed was unmade and there were abandoned items of clothing all over the floor and a mouldy smell as if the room hadn't been ventilated in ten years. I found myself getting a bit short of breath in the stale atmosphere and so I went over and opened the window. The taxi driver was waiting for me in the street below reading a paper.

What struck me about the place was that there was nothing to tell me about the person who lived there. There were no pictures on the walls no photographs or tacky holiday souvenirs, not even a postcard from a friend. I felt a heavy depression pressing down on me, shroud-like. I decided to pick up the clothes it was all I could think of to do. I collected them into a pile and then opened the wardrobe to put them inside. There were a couple of old suits hanging up, some white shirts, a pair of grey trousers and a few threadbare jumpers. On the shelves were folded T-shirts and vests, some underwear and some socks. On the floor of the wardrobe were a couple of pairs of shoes, one clean one dirty and a large cardboard box. I lifted the box out of the cupboard and set it on the floor. It was old and looked like it might fall to pieces at any moment. The top had once been taped shut, but the tape was so old that it no longer held. I raised the flap to see inside and saw that it was full of papers and packets of photographs. At last I had found the personal items I had been seeking.

I decided to take the box with me to the hospital it would give me something to do rather than just sit there and stare at my father's vacant face. I could sort through his stuff and talk to him about it as I did so. Didn't they say it was a good thing to talk to people who were in a coma? Maybe talking about things from his past might pull him back to life. I went over and shut the window and then picked up the box as carefully as I could and went downstairs.

*

The hospital was warm again, at first pleasantly so after the chill of outside, but then it became muggy and unbearable. I'd been there for an hour, talking to the man in the bed, telling him all about my life. When I couldn't think of what to say next I sat and listened to the machine that was breathing for him. Then something would occur to me and I would start talking again. After an hour I had run through my whole life story and my throat was dry. I went to the canteen and had a coffee.

When I came back I picked up the cardboard box from the floor and placed it on the bed and opened up both flaps. I didn't like to pry in his most personal possessions, but at least I was doing it in his presence, and at least I was family. Better it was me than someone else who might just throw everything out. I took a deep breath and dipped my hands into the box to see what I would find.

After an hour or so of sorting I had my father's hospital bed covered in different piles of stuff from the box. It was amazing how much one cardboard box could hold. It was the flotsam of an entire lifetime all laid out neatly before me. There was a pile for bank statements which went back several years and told me that my father had just over ten thousand pounds in savings and that the rent for his house went out on the first of every month and therefore that he didn't own his own house, the same as me.

There were some photographs from the early seventies when I was a baby of him and my mother, looking just like any other family group pictured in our back garden or on a camping holiday near the seaside somewhere. A few random shots showed my father getting slowly older over the years with an ever-changing selection of male friends in pubs or out in the countryside.

There was a small pile of letters which he had obviously deemed important enough to keep. Some were about his pension which he would be due to claim in June and there were a couple from the bank manager inviting him to come into branch to discuss the possibility of a mortgage although these letters were over ten years old and he had therefore never bothered to follow them up. There was one from an Edinburgh law firm stating that his will had been drawn up and was ready for signing, maybe he had signed it maybe he hadn't, it was something to check on if he died. I felt bad now, sorting through his stuff and thinking about his will and him still being alive lying right there beside me.

I decided it was time to return to the hospital café for something to eat. In the box I had found an old diary that looked as if it could be a hundred years old it was so tattered and dog-eared and I decided to take it with me to lunch, maybe it would tell me more about my father and give me something to talk about through the long hours of the afternoon. The doctor was due back late afternoon to talk to me once again, although I knew it would be about turning off the machines that were keeping my father alive. No doubt the hospital needed the bed.

I got my food order sorted out and sat down at a little table in the corner as far from anyone else as possible. It was still quite early and the lunchtime rush hadn't yet started. I stuck my fork into the pile of chips and fed a few into my mouth and then opened the diary that was on the table next to my can of coke.

Imagine my surprise when I saw that the diary was written in Spanish. On further investigation I realised that it wasn't my father's diary at all, but that it had belonged to my grandfather. I didn't know much at all about our family history it wasn't a subject my mother had ever wanted to broach. All I had heard was that my grandparents on my father's side had met during the Civil War in Spain and fled to England after the Nationalist victory. My grandfather had been killed in the Normandy hedgerows a couple of days after D-day in June 1944, just weeks before the birth of his son, Robert, my father.

TWENTY-THREE

By the time I had finished my chicken pie and chips lunch I had read the first few pages of the diary. Tucked inside was a hand-drawn map of Spain showing the route from Madrid down to Alicante which meant nothing to me, unless perhaps it was meant to show the route from Alicante to Madrid that my grandfather had followed the previous year when he had first been sent to the besieged Spanish capital.

The diary was for the year 1939, but there was a reference to the fall of Malaga and the death of his parents as a result of the Italian bombing in February 1937, and then there were the descriptions of life at the front in Madrid after his posting there. Every now and then there would come the mention of a brief Rebel assault that they had fought off, or the fact that an enemy shell had landed a bit too close for comfort to where they were billeted, and of course the names of those who had been killed or wounded. There was also the ever-present fear that he and his men felt of the Moors of the Foreign Legion. It was fascinating reading and I spent the afternoon engrossed in this story of the forlorn resistance of the Republican capital surrounded on three sides by General Franco's forces.

I'd been to Madrid on a couple of occasions, but I could never have imagined it as it must have been at that time. My grandfather spoke of the barricades in the streets made of rotting sandbags and bricks from the broken buildings, the shops and bars shuttered and closed. The trees that had survived the air raids had been chopped down for firewood as the city froze during that long final winter of war, its people slowly starving to death.

I knew a fair bit about the Spanish Civil War. I'd studied it at university as part of my degree, read some books about it and seen a few documentaries since, but nothing could have prepared me for this diary. It was heartbreaking to read about my grandfather's struggle in the bombed-out buildings of the Casa de Campo, to realise as he did that the Republic was now in an impossible situation after its defeat in the Battle of the Ebro and the fall of Cataluña. It was only a question of time before Madrid capitulated. I found myself wondering what had made men like my grandfather continue with the fighting even though they must have known that all hope was lost. Perhaps it was fear of Nationalist reprisals, perhaps the lingering hope that Spain might be drawn into a European war or maybe it was simply their loyalty to their Republic.

*

Sometime around mid afternoon a doctor came. He wasn't the same one from the previous day he was younger and seemed more understanding of the debate that was going through my mind. I asked him the only question that really needed to be asked. Was there really no hope of my father emerging from his coma? I mean, didn't people come out of comas after days, weeks and even years? So, why shouldn't my father?

The doctor sat down on a chair next to me and explained that my father was really already dead, it was only the machines that were breathing for him that made it seem that he was still alive. His brain had been starved of oxygen as he lay dead in the street and although the paramedics had restarted his heart it had already been too late. Sometimes people were kept in a controlled coma in intensive care to allow their brains and bodies time to heal, but that wasn't the case here.

"When the machines are switched off how long will he take to die?" I asked.

"He's already dead," whispered the doctor. "Without the machines he won't be able to breathe anymore that's all."

"So he won't suffer or anything?"

"He's not suffering now. He's already gone. Switching off the breathing apparatus just makes it official that's all."

"And what about organ donation? Isn't he too old? He was going to be sixty-five soon."

"There isn't really an age limit, we check each case individually."

"Then yes, I'd like you to use whatever you can."

"Thank you," said the doctor.

*

It was only back in my hotel room later during the night that it finally hit me that I had witnessed the death of the final member of my family and that I was all alone in the world. I had held his hand when the breathing machine had been switched off and I had stayed with him for a few moments afterwards, but then they had taken him away as speed was all important if any of his organs were to be used to help others. I didn't know if this was what he would have wanted, but it was what I would have wanted had I been in his place and therefore I went with that.

Alone in the darkness I cried myself to sleep, yes I felt sad at the death of a man I would now never get to know, but more than that I just felt so alone.

*

The next morning I told the hotel receptionist that I would be staying another night as I needed to make funeral arrangements and everything. Then I went to meet with an undertaker. Later in the morning I went back to my father's house and found his telephone book and rang his landlord and then all the other people who were listed and told them I was Robert Miller's son and that he had passed away. There weren't many, but they all expressed surprise that he had had a son. He had never mentioned me to anyone.

With the funeral arranged for a week's time, I went for a quick lunch and then returned to the house with a roll of black bin liners and emptied it of my father's possessions. Everything went into the black sacks to be thrown away. The only things I wanted to keep were already in my hotel room still in that old cardboard box.

It didn't take me long to bag up my father's meagre possessions and by mid-afternoon the job was done. The landlord came to see me and gave the house a quick once over. He said he was sorry for my loss and asked me to whom he should make out the cheque for the return of my father's deposit. I shrugged and said I guessed he should make it out to me, which he did and I gave him the keys.

At a loss for what to do, I wandered back towards the centre of Edinburgh, my collar turned up against a slanting rain that had begun to fall, and decided to go for a look around the castle. I paid for an audio guide to accompany me so that I didn't feel so alone and spent a pleasant couple of hours wandering through history. All too soon it was dark and I went for a pint and something to eat.

*

Back in London and back at work the boss sat me down in her office and asked me how things had gone. I gave her a brief account of the hospital and the switching off of the machines and told her I was going to need a few days holiday in order to attend to the funeral and everything.

She offered to fly up with me to lend her support on the day of the funeral but I told her there was no need, although I appreciated the offer. She had been at my mother's funeral the year before and I had gone to her father's a couple of years back. We had worked together for a long time although I wouldn't have said we were friends. We'd shared a drunken kiss at a work Christmas party when we were both nearly new at the company and both newly married. It had been a nice kiss, at least I'd enjoyed it, but we had never kissed again even after we were both divorced and neither of us had ever mentioned it.

*

The day after the funeral I awoke early in my hotel room to the sound of heavy rain pounding against the window. I opened the curtains and looked out onto the dreary scene in front of me. The trees were swaying alarmingly, flailing their naked branches at the sky. I showered and had breakfast, all the time my ears half listening to the rain, hoping it would stop before I had to go outside. I had one last thing to do - I had an appointment with my father's lawyer to see about the will he had made.

Although the rain didn't stop completely it did ease off a bit, and so I hurried collar up towards the centre. I knew from a previous telephone call that my father had indeed signed his will and that I was the executor, I guess he had assumed that someone would be able to track me down in the event of his death.

The lawyer's premises were small and dark and I sat waiting on an old leather sofa for a while until the right person was able to see me. An elderly man ushered me smartly into his office, pointed me to a chair opposite his desk and sat down himself. He put on his reading glasses and picked up the will from his desk and set about explaining it to me. It seems that my father hadn't been a very wealthy man, something which I already suspected. I was entitled to all his possessions and to any monies there might be in his bank account. There was no loaded secret savings account, no carefully selected investment portfolio and no forgotten country mansion. And then the lawyer dropped an unexpected bombshell.

"I have here the title deeds to your father's Spanish property," said the lawyer handing me some yellowed pieces of paper neatly folded in half.

"What?" I asked.

150

"It seems that your father acquired a place in Spain as part of the settlement of his mother Elizabeth's will when she died in 1976."

"I knew my grandmother was a nurse in Spain during the Civil War, but I didn't know she owned any property there," I said just about managing to say something despite my state of shock.

"Well, your father kept it and now it's yours."

"In what part of Spain is it?"

"You've got the document there, see what it says."

I carefully opened the deeds and looked at the Spanish wording. It was written on an old typewriter and had faded somewhat with time, but I could make out that my grandmother, Señora Elizabeth Miller, had purchased the property known as Finca El Dorado in a place called San Antonio Dos Corazones, in the Province of Alicante.

"Alicante," I informed the lawyer.

"Nice," he said and he folded his arms as if to say that our meeting was over.

"What should I do with this?" I wanted to know waving the Spanish deeds at him.

"Whatever you like," laughed the lawyer, "it's yours."

After I left the lawyer's offices I found a café not far away and sat down with a pot of tea by the window to read through the deeds of my new Spanish finca. The deed was written in the old type of formal Spanish that very few would have been able to decipher, I wondered if my father had ever had it translated since I had found no evidence of his ever having been to Spain or of his being able to speak any of the language. I had to conclude that he had just kept hold of it and had never been over to Spain to do anything about it.

There were a million thoughts racing through my mind, but uppermost was the question as to why on earth my grandmother had decided to go to Spain in the last few months of her life and purchase a property, and why Alicante? Perhaps she had planned to retire there? She had been close to retirement age in 1976 so maybe that was the reason. My grandfather had been born in the South of Spain, but if she had wanted to retire there because of his memory then surely she would have gone somewhere closer to Malaga where he had grown up? It was all very strange.

I finished my tea and headed back to my hotel to check out and get to the airport for my early afternoon flight back to London.

On the plane I thought some more about my grandmother and wondered how she had met my grandfather. Perhaps he had been wounded in the fighting around Madrid and she had nursed him back to health at the hospital, which seemed the obvious explanation. Fortunately, I had the best possible means of finding out as my grandfather's diary for 1939 was back at my house. I hadn't read much more of it, what with everything that had been going on, but I decided that as soon as I got back I would get stuck into it again and see what I could find out.

TWENTY-FOUR

Once back at home with a weekend ahead of me before going back to work on Monday I helped myself to a bottle of beer and sat down on the sofa to read some more of my grandfather's diary. The handwriting was at times difficult to decipher, no doubt he had written it in the back of troop carriers or hunched up sheltering from an enemy bombardment, and there were patches that had almost faded completely away written as it was in pencil and on poor quality paper, but the power of his words remained.

After a short while I reached the point where he began to write about the special mission that had snatched him away from Madrid just as the city had been about to surrender, and so I discovered how he had met my grandmother, Elizabeth, who had been sent along on the journey south to help with the ruse that they were just an innocent ambulance heading first to Albacete and then on to the port of Alicante. I now understood why there had been a hand drawn map of this route tucked into the diary.

The next morning after an early breakfast I picked up the diary again, eager to get to the end of the story. It must have been a terrible struggle for them to keep focused on their mission knowing that the war was lost, and of course it was impossible to imagine how terrible it must have been, knowing that they were being hunted relentlessly by an all-powerful enemy.

I wasn't too surprised when Paco, the driver, betrayed them, the times were desperate and you can understand anyone wanting to save themselves anyway they could. Even my grandfather must have known that there would be no offer of safety even if they survived as far as Alicante.

With a lump in my throat I read about the death of my grandfather's childhood friend Fernando. I couldn't begin to imagine how hard it must have been to drive away and leave his lifelong companion dead and buried by the roadside in some desolate place. That was when I think I would have given up and tried to use the lorry's special cargo for my own salvation, although of course he still had no idea what the cargo was. And then they were finally caught by the Rebel captain who had been chasing them south from Madrid.

When the lorry reached its destination so they were betrayed by the General they had risked their lives for and also they discovered that the lorry's secret cargo was stolen gold. The diary ended with their escape from the docks at Alicante and them heading further along the coast towards the last remaining Republican port of Cartagena although they were desperately short of petrol and it was extremely doubtful as to whether they could have got there or not.

There was a brief message from my grandfather on the last written page that there would be no further notes in his diary in case it fell into the wrong hands now that he had discovered the crates they had been transporting were full of something so valuable as gold. And that was the end of the story.

I was lucky enough to know a little bit more. I knew that my grandparents had escaped to England from Gibraltar, no doubt my grandmother's passport gaining them access. But there had never been any family tales of lost gold. Had they kept it a secret? My grandfather had died young in the Second World War, but my grandmother had lived on for many years. Maybe they had blown up the lorry and its cargo when they ran out of petrol somewhere on the coastal road to Cartagena. But somehow I doubted it. It wouldn't have been easy to blow up a lorry load of gold, who could do that? Whether my grandparents intended to keep the gold for themselves or whether they intended to return it to the Bank of Spain when better times came I could only guess at, but there was no way they were going to destroy it, not after what they had been through.

Had my grandmother ever told my father? If she had, why hadn't he been to Spain to find the gold for himself? Maybe she hadn't trusted him enough. I didn't really know exactly what kind of person my father had been, but he had abandoned my mother and I when we needed him most and had never tried to get in contact with me since. Had he read my grandfather's diary he would have realised precisely why his mother had hurried over to Spain as soon as General Franco was dead and bought a piece of land almost exactly half way between Alicante and Cartagena. They had obviously run out of petrol and decided to hide the gold and return for it in safer times at least that was my breath-taking conclusion. I found my heart suddenly racing, thumping so hard that I thought it might hammer its way out of my chest. It wasn't every day that one was presented with the possibility of owning a piece of land where there might be buried treasure.

The finca I had inherited certainly could be El Dorado (The Land Of Gold) as its name suggested. I was so nervous I was actually sitting on my sofa shaking with excitement.

With some controlled deep breaths I managed to calm down a bit, just enough to come to my senses and realise that the possibility that a hoard of stolen gold had remained undiscovered for seventy years was very remote indeed, still, what about Howard Carter and the lost tomb of Tutankhamun? Anything was possible.

Firstly, I needed to try to find some evidence to support my grandfather's story. Where had the gold come from in the first place? How could it have fallen into the hands of the Republican General who had ordered my grandfather to take it south? I got my laptop and searched for references to gold in the Spanish Civil War. I vaguely remembered something I had read before about the gold from the Bank of Spain being sent to Russia to pay for arms for the Republic, but I wasn't completely sure.

It didn't take too much searching around in Spanish to come up with a very definite explanation of my grandfather's gold. And the more I read about it the more scared I became that there might actually be a certain amount of truth to all of this.

At the beginning of the Civil War in 1936, Spain had the fourth largest gold reserve in the world. It was held at the Bank of Spain in the Calle Alcalá in the centre of Madrid and was estimated to have been worth US$788 million.

When Madrid was attacked by the Rebels in the first year of the war and the long siege began, it was decided to transfer most of the gold out of the Spanish capital for safe keeping. The task fell to the Republican Minister of Finance, Dr Juan Negrín, who was later to be the Republic's last Prime Minister. He arranged for the gold to be taken to the port of Cartagena where it was to be loaded onto a Russian ship.

A fleet of lorries arrived at the Bank of Spain and 7,900 bags of gold coins were loaded onto them, worth around US$500 million. New drivers were then brought in and told that they were transporting explosives and the lorries headed for the Atocha railway station. The gold was then taken by train to Cartagena where it was kept in a heavily-guarded cave until being loaded onto a Russian ship.

There is some debate as to whether the gold was really meant to end up in Russia or not, some people think that it was supposed to be taken to a port in Southern France. Whatever the intended destination, the ship found its way to the Black Sea port of Odessa, from where the gold was transferred to Moscow.

Stalin, once he had his hands on Spain's gold, never intended for it to be returned, and by the end of the Second World War it had all been spent in the fight against Hitler's Germany.

The rest of Spain's gold reserve was finally transferred to France and exchanged into currency in order to buy arms to continue the resistance against Franco, in the forlorn hope that Britain and France might yet end their policy of non-intervention and come to the Republic's aid before it was too late.

The really interesting fact that I managed to uncover was that when the 'Moscow Gold' was recounted, there were found to be 7,800 bags, a hundred less than had originally left the Bank of Spain. So the mystery was obviously what had happened to those 100 bags of gold coins, Louis d'Or, Sovereigns, Dollars and gold Pesetas.

I spent the rest of the weekend trying to convince myself that the story just couldn't be true. At times I felt I was succeeding, but then the phrase 'what if...?' would come back into my mind. What if the General had managed to keep back 100 bags of coins from the Russians? What if he really had placed it in an American ambulance for it to be taken to Alicante? What if my grandfather really had driven away from the port and run out of petrol and buried the gold on abandoned farmland? What if that farmland now belonged to me?

Sunday night I couldn't sleep a wink. In the end, I got up an hour before my alarm was due to go off and printed off a letter of resignation from my job. Maybe it does sound like a hasty thing to do, but the more I had thought about it, the more convinced I had become that this was the right thing to do. It wasn't just about the gold. It was also about me. I was nudging forty and my life was going nowhere, I had no wife, no children, I didn't own my own house and so I had nothing to tie me down. Here I had been presented with the opportunity for a great adventure and I was determined to grasp it with both hands.

Once I had worked out my notice I had decided I would fly to Madrid, to start the journey for the lost gold in the Spanish capital, just as my grandfather's journey had begun seventy years before. I wanted to hire a car and follow the diary's route south towards Albacete and Alicante. And then of course I could set about finding the finca that had come into my possession and discover if there really was any gold hidden there. Even if there wasn't any buried treasure it was still going to be the adventure of a lifetime, and it would do me the power of good to start a new life somewhere else. I had the money that my wife and her new man had paid me for our house and although it wasn't a fortune, when combined with my savings and the money I had just inherited from my father, I had plenty to live on for a while. In Spain I could probably live for several years before I had to worry about having an income, which gave me plenty of time to figure out what I wanted to do with my life. If things didn't work out then I could always go back to my job or look for another translation firm.

In the back of my mind I had the idea of building myself a little house on the land I had inherited, but I wasn't sure if I had enough money for that or even if I would be given permission to do so. I would just have to wait and see. There were so many questions bombing around my brain and it felt good not to have all the answers. I was looking forward to being there already.

*

I got to work ahead of everyone else as always and waited for the boss to arrive. She was a little later than usual since there had been a brief flurry of snow and cars were crawling along in the treacherous conditions. That was one thing I wasn't going to miss I thought to myself, London in the snow. I asked my boss if she had a moment for a brief chat sometime in the morning and she said she'd give me a call as soon as she had allocated work to everyone. I felt my resignation letter burning a hole through my jacket pocket desperate to get out.

I took my coffee to my desk and set about finishing a couple of things I had left from before my latest trip to Edinburgh, just enough to tide me over until a new piece of work came my way. All the while I was rehearsing in my mind exactly what I was going to say to the boss.

After an hour or so the phone rang and the boss said I could go through. I took a couple of deep breaths and headed for her little office. No sooner had I sat down than she beat me to it.

"Listen Daniel, I've got some bad news." I couldn't remember the last time she had called me Daniel and not Danny. "I've been worrying all weekend about how to tell you, but there isn't a nice way to do it, so I'm just going to come straight out with it." She gave a loud sigh and looked out of her window. "You're going to be made redundant. I'm terribly, terribly sorry. It was nothing to do with me it's come from Head Office. We've got to lose two members of staff and I'm afraid you're one of them. You know there's a recession on and that everyone is cutting back at the moment."

"I see," I said, a bit shocked.

"You've been here the longest and your salary is the highest, well, apart from mine of course, that's why you've been chosen."

"Okay," I said, nodding slowly as the information she had dealt me slowly filtered through my brain. The resignation letter in my pocket was no longer burning to get out in fact it felt positively icy in there.

"Someone is coming from Head Office to talk to you tomorrow, you know, work out a compensation package and everything."

"Compensation?"

"Yes, of course, you'll get paid something for every year you've been working here."

"Really? How much?"

"They'll let you know tomorrow. I'm really sorry to have to be the one to tell you about this, just after your father's death and everything. Like I said it was nothing to do with me."

I didn't care whether she was lying or not, although I suspected that Head Office wouldn't just fire me without her approval, the only thing I could think of was that I was going to be paid some money when I had been about to jack in my job anyway.

My boss was looking at me kind of awkwardly and I realised that the situation was getting embarrassing for her.

"Thanks for telling me," I said and I got up to leave.

158

"If you need a reference or anything don't hesitate to ask. I'm sure you can find another job soon enough."

I wanted to tell her that she had just made me a very happy man and that I was planning to go to Spain, but I decided to wait until my severance package was all signed before I let on that she had actually done me a favour. I got up to leave and she suddenly remembered that it was me who had asked for a meeting with her.

"I'm sorry. There was something you wanted to talk to me about wasn't there?" she said.

"Oh, don't worry, it's not important now." I left her office and I guess she thought I had meant to ask for a pay rise or something. I quickly pushed my resignation letter into the office shredder before it slipped out of my pocket or something.

TWENTY-FIVE

I braced myself slightly as the plane dropped in an ungainly manner towards the runway. There was a sudden jolt and the back wheels were down. That was it, I had landed in Madrid. After slow torturous weeks of waiting I was finally here. My great adventure was about to begin. I looked out through the window and saw Spain at last. It was of course International-Airport-Spain, but Spain nonetheless.

I didn't have any luggage to collect as I had travelled with just a small carryon case, just the bare minimum of possessions carried forward from my old life. I had managed to persuade my ex-wife to look after a couple of boxes of things for me until I could get settled in Spain, I'd even left her a cheque to cover the expense of sending them over as soon as I had an address to send them to. Not surprisingly there had been no emotional goodbye. I think she was relieved that I was leaving the country. She was getting stuck into her second chance with her new man and her new baby and was glad to see me go.

There had been no great farewell at work either, just a quick round of beers after my last day and then everyone had made excuses and left early. The boss had stayed for a while longer than the rest but it was obvious she felt uncomfortable being there. I decided I'd had enough and she seemed relieved when I told her I had some urgent packing to do at home. She kissed me on the cheek and hurried away, we both knew we would never see each other again, although she had said she would love to come over to Spain and I had said that she would be very welcome.

I picked up my hire car and took a deep breath before heading out of the car park to drive on the wrong side of the road for the first time in years. I kept my right hand on the gear stick and moved out into the fast-flowing mid-afternoon traffic. I was lucky that I didn't have to drive across Madrid or anything, since from Barajas Airport I was quite close to the link road to the A3 motorway.

*

On 1930s Spanish roads my grandfather's journey would have been totally different from a modern-day trip. Add to that the fact that they had been told to avoid the main roads and only travel at night and you could begin to understand why the heavily-laden, slow-moving

160

ambulance had taken so long to travel south. But in modern times on the motorway I made good progress in my nearly-new red Ford Fiesta. I reached the turn off for my first destination in just over an hour. I had booked a night in a small Hostal in the town of Fuentidueña de Tajo where I wanted to see the iron bridge over the river. This was the place where my grandfather had been chased by the local communist militia and had escaped by blowing up a section of the bridge with dynamite.

Once I had checked in at the hostal and had a quick shower in my room I set off through the town down towards the river. It was a cold but fine day and as I approached the river I felt a strong breeze rise up around me making me feel truly alive. I knew from the internet that the iron bridge had been built by Gustave Eiffel no less, and had been completed in 1871. It had been restored in 2001 so I wasn't too surprised to find no signs of any damage as I walked across. It was amazing to think that I was in a place where my grandfather had been so long before me. Here his quick thinking had saved not only his life, but the lives of those with him on his mission. I wondered how I would have reacted had I been in his situation, but it was impossible to tell. I was grateful that I came from a generation that had not known the horrors of war at first hand. It was difficult to imagine the fear that must have gripped these people as they made their way towards the coast. In our modern times with so much information at our fingertips it is difficult to imagine a period when people had little idea what was happening in the next town let alone in the rest of the country.

I sat on the bank of the river and looked at the bridge, feeling slightly numb from the cold but feeling happy nonetheless. And there I remained, alone with my thoughts, until it started to get dark. Back up in the town I had a quick beer and a couple of tapas in a bar by the main square, and looking out through the large window I could see the Town Hall and the tall clock tower next to it both beautifully illuminated. I didn't stay long. I've never felt comfortable in a bar on my own and more so here where I felt as if everyone else was watching me. Maybe they didn't see many foreigners here or maybe I was just being paranoid, but either way I was soon back in my room at the hostal.

*

The next morning I had an early breakfast in another bar, this one almost empty and then set off on the drive to Albacete. Had I stuck to the motorway I would have been there in no time at all since the distance was only some 200km, but I wanted to take the same route that my grandfather had travelled through the sierras. And so I left the motorway at Viñas-Viejas and headed for the lake where I hoped to see the old farm where they had parked up for the day.

I soon came to the water and the road skirted around it. I kept my eyes peeled for the ruins of an old farm house, but there was nothing. When I had gone half way around I pulled over to the roadside and got out to have a walk. The air was fresh, decidedly chilly. I guessed that the water in the lake wasn't much above freezing as it was melt water from the nearby mountains. The first thaw of an early spring had recently begun. I had to conclude that the water level was now much higher than it had been at the time of the Civil War, and that the old abandoned farm had long ago been submerged. I sat down by the shore and looked across the snaking surface of the lake and tried to imagine my grandmother bathing there and her terror when she realised that an enemy plane was fast approaching.

I stayed for some time, just thinking about where my life might be going and making a few plans and then unmaking them again. It was impossible to know what was going to become of my life in the coming months and I liked that uncertainty in a strange way. It was good that every hour bought a new experience after so many years of sameness. Here I was on an adventure I could never have imagined a year or two ago.

Somewhat reluctantly I returned to my car and put the heater on to warm me up, especially my hands. When I was more or less thawed out I set off again along the small road around the lake, scaring flocks of birds up from the water as I went. It was a beautiful if somewhat isolated place, misty, cold almost eerie, the mountains in the background covered still with a fine layer of snow.

Somewhere further along the road I saw up ahead the high white wall of a village cemetery and suddenly realised that this was where my grandfather had come across the local villagers in the process of shooting some of their communist neighbours. I pulled over and got out for a quick look. I walked over towards the wall and inspected it for bullet holes, but although it hadn't been painted for several years it had obviously been repaired at some stage since the war, no doubt to hide its shameful secret. How many such places of execution must there have been across Spain during the Civil War and the years of persecution that followed immediately afterwards? Almost certainly every town and village had somewhere like this, where heinous assassinations had taken place beneath an uncaring moon. Half a generation had simply been executed without trial. Often, their only crime was having been caught on the wrong side when the Rebel uprising began. There had been priests and nuns shot for religious reasons and intellectuals such as teachers and writers just because they were considered a threat to a common-people's regime. They even shot the poet Lorca.

I drove away from the village cemetery and soon hooked up with a new road that took me through the Sierra del Pintado on the way towards Belmonte. My grandfather had not actually been to Belmonte of course, they had just crossed the main road about four kilometres to the north which was where they had punctured a tyre and driven into a ditch. But, I had seen the spectacular castle on the internet whilst planning my route and thought it would be worth a small detour. I had always been fascinated by castles since I was a boy and the fact that the lorry's route south had taken them past so many old medieval castles had been one of my reasons for taking this drive down from Madrid rather than flying directly from England to Alicante. I could have lunch in Belmonte too and then drive on towards Albacete in the afternoon.

*

The castle in Belmonte was breathtaking perched up on top of a hill overlooking the village. It was straight out of some fairytale with its round stone turrets and carefully-shaped battlements. I left my car down in the village and walked up the hill to take a closer look. I had a little notebook with me with details of things to see en route during my trip, and I had written that work on the castle began in 1456 and it was somewhat hastily finished in preparation for the civil war of 1475-80. Later, in the nineteenth century, it was the residence of la Condesa de Teba, Eugenia de Montijo, who married Napoleon III and became Empress of France. I did a tour with an audio guide and then went back

163

down to the village to look for a restaurant. I wanted to try a local lamb dish if I could find a place with one on the menu.

*

In the afternoon I pressed ahead for the main road to Albacete. I had booked myself into the Gran Hotel in the Plaza Altozano where my grandparents had rested for a few hours and eaten a frugal meal, and I wanted to get there in order to have a bit of a rest. This journey had been emotionally tiring so far and I wanted a shower and a bit of a sleep. My lunch sat heavily on my stomach and the sun through the windscreen warmed my face in an unaccustomed way. I by-passed the village of San Clemente and joined the main N-301 road at Minaya, from where it was only about forty kilometres to Albacete.

The Gran Hotel was certainly an impressive building with its blue-tiled turrets and ornate balconies. I could imagine the effect it must have had upon my grandmother to see such unexpected splendour in the midst of a desperate war. It must have reminded her of better times.

Albacete had been of course the main base for the International Brigades. For many of the thirty thousand or so young men who had come to Spain to fight fascism it was here in Albacete where they received the only military training they would ever have. If they were lucky they might even have been instructed on how to fire one of the obsolete Russian rifles that they were likely be given to take into battle. For all the gold that arrived in Moscow, the Spanish Republic received very poor quality goods in exchange.

After a rest in my hotel room I went for a walk through the streets harassed by a cold wind that swept in from the plains. The air was flecked with snow and the chill tore at my throat like icy knives. I must confess that I was looking forward to reaching the Mediterranean coast the next day and escaping the last of the winter up here on the plain. When I could take no more and my face was numb with cold I went into a little restaurant to save myself from frostbite.

Walking back to the hotel I saw it all lit up, and even though it was now raining and the night was dark and miserable, I had to pause to take in the sight. I walked slowly across the little square with its manicured bushes and rain-soaked benches and then gratefully tumbled into the warmth of the hotel lobby. Up in my room I headed for a long hot shower, the steam filling the little bathroom like a thick warm fog. I stayed under the shower for an age, letting myself defrost until I felt alive once more. Then I lay on my bed watching the news on TV until I felt sleep creeping up on me at last.

TWENTY-SIX

When I awoke in the Gran Hotel in Albacete I went down for breakfast. Okay, the dining room had probably changed beyond all recognition from how it had been back in March 1939, it might even have been in a different part of the hotel back then, but I still felt a strong sense of being close to my grandparents. At this hotel they had been served a meal by a waiter, despite the fact that the city was only hours away from surrender and there was the danger of a bombing raid at any moment. It must have been a very surreal experience. I had my breakfast alone surrounded by mirrors.

Back in my car I was soon out of Albacete and started on the final leg of my journey which would take me to Alicante. There were some castles to see en route at Chinchilla de Monte-Aragón, Almansa and Villena. Also, I would drive past the reservoir where Paco, the driver of the ambulance, had tried to shoot the others and surrender the gold to the advancing Rebels. And of course there was the place where my grandfather had buried his childhood friend Fernando. I knew it wasn't far from Almansa, just after the fork in the road where the old N-430 headed for Valencia whilst the old N-330 turned towards Alicante. They were now motorways with different names.

I found a turn in by the reservoir just before Almansa and got out of the car to have a look at the scenery. There was a huge curved dam holding the water at bay as it had been since 1584 when it was built and, beyond, the spectacular scenery of the Sierra del Mugrón. I didn't stay long, just a matter of minutes to take in the view and give a thought to Paco, the driver, who had lost his life somewhere near here, shot by an English nurse. They had been desperate times and his willingness to betray this final mission was understandable in a way. He had little or no hope of being able to go back to his life from before the war, and no faith in his own side's ability to get him to safety. Add to that the fact that the ambulance was almost out of petrol by this stage of their journey and so he took the only option that remained available to him, to try to make a deal with the enemy and save his own life.

In the village of Almansa, just under a hundred kilometres from Alicante, I walked up a steep slope to visit the spectacular fourteenth

166

century castle perched high on a rocky outcrop from where it completely dominated the village and the surrounding countryside. Almansa had been of great strategic importance in medieval times because of its position as a pass on the route to Valencia. There had also been a great battle fought in the area in 1707 during the War of Spanish Succession.

The castle closed at one o'clock during the week, and so I was back in my car heading away from the village looking for the spot where the escaping ambulance had finally run out of petrol and been caught up by the Rebel captain who had been pursuing them all the way from Madrid. Less than ten kilometres from Almansa came the merging of the two motorways, and I headed for Alicante, just as the ambulance laden with gold had done seventy years before. And then came the moment when they had finally run out of petrol.

My grandfather's diary said they had coasted down a slope and come to a standstill when the road levelled out. I pulled over and got out for a quick look around although the road was busy and cars and lorries were thundering past at regular intervals. I just wanted to see where Fernando's final resting place could have been, but it was soon evident that where he had been buried must have been where the road now ran, as it had been made into a dual-carriageway in more modern times and later still widened into the A-31 motorway. I quickly returned to my car and got back into the stream heading for the coast. It was the only disappointing moment of my trip so far. I had imagined that it would have been a desolate and lonely place, somewhere peaceful and untouched by modern life, but of course it was anything but that, with thousands of motor vehicles thundering past every day.

*

My next stop was for lunch and to visit another castle, this time at Villena where the Moors had begun to build fortifications in the twelfth century. This castle had two tiers of walls with a tall slim keep inside, from the top of which there was a spectacular view of the town laid out below with the church of Santiago at its centre.

I didn't spend too long there as I was now impatient to get to Alicante where I had booked my final hotel for the trip and where I would part company with my hire car. The A-31 motorway took me to the southern approach to the city which was the same way the ambulance would have arrived.

It was late afternoon by the time I had sorted myself out in Alicante. The temperature had risen dramatically for me compared to the previous evening in Albacete. From my hotel it was a short walk to the beach where I stood and looked at the sea with the luxury of sand beneath my feet. I could imagine what it must be like in the height of the summer season covered in boiling bodies, the smell of coconut sunscreen and the noise of thousands of people all talking at once. On top of the hill completely dominating the city, as it had done since the fourteenth century, was the Santa Barbara castle, watching over the port below. The port was filled with small weekend sailing boats, their masts rattling in the gentle breeze. How different it was today from those terrible final hours of the civil war back in March 1939. Here thousands of people had finally had to face the fact that there was no possibility of rescue from their dying Republic. There had been many who had committed suicide rather than face imprisonment at the hands of the victors and many more who had been herded into quickly established concentration camps and worked and starved to death. It is estimated that there were around 100,000 executions carried out after the end of the war, but there were many who died from beatings and neglect whilst in prison.

*

The next morning I took the *cercanías* train to Elche from where I was able to get a bus to my final destination of San Antonio Dos Corazones. The bus route went past the protected wetlands of the Parque Natural de El Hondo to Los Rosales, and from there it was just a further ten minutes up the road to San Antonio. The bus stopped in a little central square and I got off behind a couple of old women and stood there wondering what to do. The bus drove away. I hadn't imagined that it would be a big place, there was hardly any mention of it on the internet, I hadn't been able to find a hotel or anything, but this had to be one of the smallest places I'd ever seen.

The two old women hurried away across the square and left me alone. There were some palm trees around the square to offer some shade and I went and sat on a bench under one of them in order to have a bit of a think. In the end I walked over to a bar in the corner of the square. There was always someone in a bar who knew the answer to any question you might have.

There were two old men sitting at a table in a dark corner drinking coffee and the elderly owner leaning on the bar watching daytime TV on a small set on a shelf just above the two customers' heads. I wished everyone a good morning and ordered myself a white coffee. When the barman placed it on the counter before me I asked him if there was anywhere to stay in the village. He told me there was a small *venta* just outside of the village and they had some rooms which they let to tourists in the summer, otherwise I would have to go back to Los Rosales where there were a couple of small *pensiones*. All in all it didn't sound too promising, still if the *venta* would let me have a room, even though it was out of season, at least I would be closer to my plot of land when I eventually found it. I didn't fancy having to catch the bus back and forth from Los Rosales every day it would be far easier to be based in the village. That way I could start to get to know a few people. If there was someone of my own age they might even welcome a friend here in this lost little place. I couldn't imagine that San Antonio had changed much since the 1930s. Had my grandfather really driven the ambulance through this tiny place? Maybe the engine was already spluttering as it began to run out of fuel. Was he desperately looking for somewhere to hide his valuable cargo and had headed inland away from the coastal road?

I finished my coffee, paid and said goodbye. The owner bid me *vaya con Diós*, no doubt assuming that he would never see me in his tiny forgotten bar again. He couldn't know that I was planning to stick around for a while. I crossed the deserted square and headed along the main road in the same direction that the bus had gone when it had left me behind. There were a few single-storey houses and a small shop that seemed to be the only one in town and then I was out into the dusty countryside. In the distance I could make out a cluster of four tall pine trees, and below in the shade the red/brown tiles of the roof of the Venta El Quinto Pino which the barman had told me about. It was nearly midday and the sun was high in a cloudless sky, the pure blueness of which you would never see in England. It was warm and I began to sweat as I walked away from the village on the shimmering tarmac of the road, pulling my little case behind me.

The English have an image abroad as being slightly eccentric, and I could only hope that no one would see me as I trudged through the heat towards the *venta*, my face red and sweaty, my little blue suitcase causing a stir in the dust. It wasn't the way I had planned to arrive. A white van rushed from the village and blew past in a blast of warm air that took my breath away.

Suddenly, just a little further up the road the van screeched to a halt in a billowing cloud of dust. As I watched in amazement the reversing light came on and it was suddenly backing along the road towards me almost as fast as it had rocketed away. I moved over to the side of the road as a precaution, but the driver slammed the brakes on hard when he was close by causing another dust storm. An electric window opened and the driver leaned across the passenger seat to shout at me. I hoped he hadn't bothered to stop to ask for directions.

"Are you going to the Quinto Pino?" he asked.

"Yes," I replied.

"Hop in, I've got a delivery for them, it'll save you the walk."

The man wasn't offering, he was telling me that I was going to be taken there in his van. At least I would now arrive in more style than I had anticipated. I opened the door and climbed in pulling my suitcase up onto my lap. I had barely shut the door than we were on our way.

"Where are you from?" shouted the man trying to make his voice heard over the roar of the engine and the blare of the radio.

"England," I shouted back.

"Welcome to Spain Englishman," he laughed and he took a hand off the steering wheel and offered it to me to shake. "Manolo," he stated.

"Danny" I told him, shaking the hand he had offered. A minute later we hurtled into the car park in front of the *venta* and shuddered to a halt by some arches through which I could see tables and chairs already set out for lunch.

"Who should I see about a room?" I asked Manolo.

"I should talk to Carmen, she's nice, you'll like her. Let me introduce you." He opened the back of his van and took out a sack of loaves of bread and headed for the veranda where the tables and chairs were and shouted out for Carmen a couple of times at the top of his voice. A woman emerged from within the restaurant area drying her hands on a tea towel. She looked about mid thirties, long brown hair, wavy, slightly lighter in colour than most Spanish women. She smiled at Monolo and then looked past him at me. Something about her eyes made me nervous and I suddenly found myself wishing the ground would just open up and swallow me.

"Who's this?" she asked Manolo.

"He's an *extranjero* I picked up near the village. He was walking here to ask about a room," the bread man told her.

"We don't rent out rooms in the winter," she said, "it's not worth it for one night."

Manolo turned to face me and gave an apologetic shrug.

"Sorry *señor* she says they don't rent out rooms in the winter. If you like you can come with me and I'll find you somewhere in Los Rosales, I'm delivering there next."

I hadn't been able to speak so far in the presence of this woman for some reason which I couldn't begin to explain, but I knew at that moment the thing I wanted most in the world was to stay at that isolated *venta* for the foreseeable future. From somewhere deep inside I felt a surge of self-confidence I had never experienced before and I turned to Carmen.

"I'm not just here for one night," I told her. "I want to stay for a while, a month at least."

"A Month?" she asked disbelievingly, no one had ever stayed at El Quinto Pino for a month before, not even in the summer. "Why?"

I quickly unzipped my suitcase and pulled out a plastic document file and searched for the deeds to my newly-inherited piece of land. Carmen and Manolo watched me with interest, no doubt wondering what on earth I could be looking for. At last I found it and waved it at the woman with a flourish.

"I'm here because of this," I informed them triumphantly. "My father died last month and I inherited a piece of land near here. Take a look." I held out the deeds towards Carmen who took them from me cautiously and studied them for a second or two.

"A month you say?" she said.

"At least," I responded, a bit breathless after the most frightening conversation I had ever had in Spanish. She handed the deeds back to me

171

and looked into my eyes. I suddenly felt weak and started to wish I had just taken Manolo up on his offer of a lift to Los Rosales. I hated all this new-found confusion that was coursing around inside me.

"I'll talk to Antonio," she decided at last, "see what he says." She turned and walked away back through the restaurant.

"Don't worry," Manolo said, "you're as good as in already."

"Yes?"

"Yes. Antonio will do whatever Carmen suggests. She twists men around her little finger that one," he laughed waving his little finger at me and almost dropping his sack of bread. I think I knew what he meant.

TWENTY-SEVEN

Alone in my room at last, I sat down on the lumpy double bed and breathed a huge sigh of relief. Relief that I was away from Carmen for a while and relief that I had somewhere I could call home again. Being a person of fixed habits, almost bordering on routines, this trip had been very difficult for me. Every hour had brought with it a completely new experience, and whilst I had battled with my inner cowardice I had ignored the fact that I was basically homeless. Now I had somewhere to stay, for at least a month, perhaps longer if I needed it and didn't cause them any problems, which I didn't intend to.

It wasn't much of a home. It was the size of a small study with a double bed, bedside table, wardrobe, desk and chair all crowded into it. Carmen had promised me it was the best room they had, so I really wouldn't have wanted to see one of the others, no wonder people didn't stay here too long. But for me it was as if a great burden had been lifted from my shoulders. I had somewhere to unpack my things, a wardrobe to hang my few clothes in and a desk to lay my papers out on.

Of course I didn't have much stuff, but it was all I had after all. I put my diary on the desk with my grandfather's civil war one beside it. I had decided to write down my adventures just as he had done, and I had completed a couple of pages already about my journey down from Madrid. Then there was my document file with the deeds to the Finca El Dorado, my father's and my grandmother's wills with translations into Spanish stamped and signed by my old boss although I had done them myself, my passport, my birth certificate and my qualification certificates. I also had a reference from my boss with a translation in Spanish, which was slightly more praising of my qualities than the original, since I had written the translation myself and got the boss to sign it. The only other thing I had to put on my new desk was Laurie Lee's *Red Sky at Sunrise* which was the one book that I owned that I hadn't been able to leave behind in the boxes with my ex-wife. I had read it twenty times at least and it was nearly as dog-eared as my grandfather's diary from 1939, but it was the only book I knew I could read over and over again and never tire of. Quite often when I reached the end of the third part of the book I would simply turn back to the front and start all over again.

Beside the bed on the far side was a door that led through to a tiny bathroom. Well, bathroom was a bit of a misnomer since there was no bath, just a shower, toilet and wash basin. I got up off the bed and took my wash bag through to the other room and set out my toothbrush and paste and shaving equipment on a glass shelf above the basin. There was no shampoo or gel in the shower and I would have to remember to get some. There were no towels either although Carmen had promised to find some for me after lunch. And lunch seemed like a good idea just then.

*

I had planned to set off in search of my little piece of land after lunch, but the *menú del día* included wine and Carmen had just left a bottle on my table rather than pour me a glass. I had a salad plastered with white wine vinegar and virgin olive oil and then a plate of *paella*. This was the El Quinto Pino's speciality, so Carmen informed me. Antonio the owner, who was also the chef, was famous for his *paella* for miles around. And it had to be true because the dining room was soon full and people were forced out onto the covered terrace.

After I finished eating I went over to the bar and had a coffee whilst I waited for Carmen to finish serving tables so that she could get me some towels. I planned to have a quick shower and then head off in search of the Finca El Dorado, maybe Antonio would know where it was. In the end I had a quick shower laid down on my bed and fell asleep.

By the time I woke up, most of the afternoon had passed me by. I could hear noise from the bar below and went down to investigate. I found Antonio behind the bar watching a re-run of some recent football game on the big TV, with a group of lively old men playing dominoes to while away the afternoon. I sat on a bar stool next to the counter and ordered a coffee and then showed Antonio the deeds to my grandmother's land. He studied the document carefully for a minute or two and then took it over to the group of old men and got them to inspect it. One of the men seemed to know something about it and looked over at me. He waved his hand to beckon me across.

It turned out that the land called the Finca El Dorado was referred to locally as Finca la Inglesa because it had been bought many years before by a mysterious English woman who had never been seen again. The old man explained that the land had been abandoned since before the civil war when the old farmer who had lived there had died with no one to pass it on to. During the war it had been collectivised like all the farmland around and then afterwards it had just become the property of the Ayuntamiento de Rosales until it had been purchased from them not long after the death of Franco by my grandmother.

The man told me that it was a couple of kilometres further out of town along the same road as the Venta El Quinto Pino and that it was just off a big bend. I would know it because there were a couple of tall plane trees and it was completely overgrown. I thanked the man, finished my coffee and set off up the road.

It was cooler now in the late evening, the shadows of the trees were starting to stretch lazily across the road and the sky was turning golden. I walked quickly as I wanted to get there and back before nightfall. I was soon breathing heavily since it had been a long time since I had done any real exercise and I was just beginning to think about turning back and waiting until the morning when up ahead I caught a glimpse of two tall plane trees. I hurried on and soon saw the bend in the road and beyond it the tangled mess of overgrown vegetation that had taken over the land in the last eighty years.

I don't really know what I had expected to find. I hadn't thought it would be a neat and tidy little farm, but on the other hand I was surprised by its state of total abandonment. It was obvious that the Ayuntamiento of Los Rosales had never bothered to keep an eye on it and they probably couldn't believe their luck when some strange foreign woman turned up out of the blue and insisted on buying it.

If I had thought that I might stroll across my land looking for possible clues as to where the gold might be hidden then I was very much mistaken. I stood for a while just looking at the absolute mess around me and feeling depressed. Then I turned around and set off back towards the Venta. Occasionally a car or van would pass by, but otherwise I was alone walking through the gloom. I was relieved to see the lights of the Quinto Pino up ahead welcoming me back.

The next morning after breakfast I caught the bus into Los Rosales to change the land into my name. The bus stopped at the Venta El Quinto Pino if you stood in the road and waved at the driver as Antonio showed me. On the way back I only had to mention to the driver that I wanted to be dropped off there and I wouldn't have to walk out from town.

I soon realised that my visit to the Land Registry Office was not going to be a quick one. I was passed around from person to person until I was sent back to the first person I had seen. In the end he gave an apologetic shrug and said that if I left my paperwork with him he would take a look at it and give me a call as to when I should come back. I told him it was urgent and he gave a sad smile and indicated the mountain of abandoned files that took up the right hand side of his very large desk. In the end I gave him the number of the Venta and told him he could leave a message there for me.

I needed an ID number if I was going to stay in Spain so I went to the Police Station to find out about that. They told me that ID cards were no longer issued to foreigners but instead I would be given a residence certificate with my ID number on it. When I asked for one I was told that I needed a Social Security number first. I was directed across town to the Social Security Office. After a long wait to see the right person I was told that they couldn't issue me with a Social Security number until I had an ID number. It appeared that I was trapped in some sort of vicious circle, but there had to be a way around it somehow, surely I wasn't the first foreign person to want to live in Spain? I trudged wearily back across town and found the foreigners department at the Police Station had closed for lunch.

I caught the bus back in a foul mood knowing that I had achieved nothing and that I had simply been humiliated by the evil workings of the Spanish bureaucratic system. I would have to try again the next day.

The next morning I got the early bus with a steely determination in my heart. At the Police Station I discovered that I needed a temporary ID number that I could use to get a Social Security number which would then allow me to get a real ID number. The whole morning slipped quietly away in walking back and forth across town, waiting patiently in non-moving queues and a quick dash to the bank to pay the necessary fees involved. Spanish people could pay in cash in the Police Station but foreigners were required to visit the bank and then rejoin the back of the queue once they got back to the Police Station.

I handed in the bank receipt, along with the required forms and a photocopy of my passport and was told to come back the next day to pick up my certificate. When I pressed the guy about that and the fact that I had already spent two whole mornings running round in circles he eventually gave in, clicked on the print button on his computer and my green certificate emerged with the all important number. Another day I would set about changing my driver's licence to a Spanish one, but I felt I needed a few days break from paperwork it was doing my head in.

I got off the bus in the village this time and had some *tapas* at the little bar in the main square. I felt I needed a break from Carmen too. I found her presence unnerving to say the least and was a bit fed up of always being so tongue-tied around her. My spoken Spanish, which was slowly coming back to me day by day, seemed to stumble and falter in her presence so that I was convinced that she must think me some kind of mumbling idiot. I found her harder to understand too as she was from Andalucía and didn't have the same accent as the locals, she talked faster than they did as well and never said the Ss in her words. I was accustomed for example to the D being omitted from words like *pescado* which became *pescao* that was normal across most of Spain, but when Carmen was delivering the Venta's lunchtime menu the word for fish got reduced to just *pecao*.

The *tapas* were good and I helped them down with a couple of cool beers and then went and sat in the square in the shade of a palm tree to wait for the heat of midday to subside a bit more before walking back to the Venta.

About an hour later I was half way out from the village, my head bowed, trudging along in my own personal dust cloud when I heard an approaching bicycle. I looked up and saw Carmen riding towards me obviously having finished her lunchtime stint at the Venta. She smiled when she saw me and slowed down.

"Hey there," she said, "the bus stops at the Venta you know."

"Yes, I know, I had some *tapas* in the village for a change."

"We missed you at dinnertime," she called out as she cycled away and I turned and waved after her. Did she really just say that she had missed me at dinnertime? I realised that my heart was pounding fit to burst out of my chest. She had done it to me again, left me all flustered and nervous. Why did it always have to happen? She hadn't really missed me at dinnertime it was just something she had thought of to say on the spur of the moment and it had left me all weak at the knees as if I were some kind of love-struck teenager. I really hoped I wasn't falling in love with her, nothing good was ever going to come of that. She was way out of my league. In fact, I probably wasn't even good enough to get into any league let alone hers'.

A bicycle might be a good idea I thought as I walked on, not for getting to and from the village as it wasn't really very far, but for me to get out to the Finca El Dorado. I had only been there once, but after a brief rest at the Venta I had another visit planned for the afternoon. I had been thinking about getting an old car to run around in, once I had changed my driver's licence, but a bicycle would make me fitter, although a car would still be a good idea in order to take equipment and stuff that I would need to buy in Los Rosales.

TWENTY-EIGHT

By the time I had been in Spain a month, I had begun to feel a bit more at ease. The Land Registry Office had finally called and I now had the deeds to the land in my name, which meant I could think about what to do with the land, and how to set about looking for the hidden Republican gold, if indeed there was any. The first thing was to cut back the mass of vegetation that had been left to grow wild for so long and to put up some kind of fence to show that the land now had an owner and hopefully to deter people from entering.

Manolo, the bread delivery man, had found me a car, and I was now the proud owner of an ancient, grey, old-style Ibiza that had belonged to some old farmer for donkey's years and was used to country lanes and dirt tracks. Manolo said it was a complete pile of useless shit that no one else would dare to touch and that it would be just perfect for me. I took it to the little garage on the other side of the village out on the road to Los Rosales and after a quick once over the mechanic pronounced it to be a complete pile of useless shit, just as Manolo had promised. It was exactly what I needed to keep my tools in and to get me to and from the Finca El Dorado.

And so I began, ever so slowly, to clear the land. It was a huge plot, well over 5,000m², running back from the bend in the road, sloping down towards a stream. It was bordered on either side by other smaller fincas that were immaculately tidy and planted with fruit trees, neat rows of vines and assorted vegetables. That was how I liked to envisage my land some day.

I used a machete to cut back giant thorn bushes which had evil barbs that still managed to stab my hands even through a thick pair of gloves, and I had an industrial strimmer to get through the tall grass and towering weeds. It was slow going, but then I wasn't in a rush or anything. I would get up early, as soon as I heard the first sounds of the coffee machine in the bar below my room and have a quick breakfast before driving out to work on the land.

The days were starting to lengthen and felt ever warmer as spring began to think about its annual metamorphosis into summer, and so, by midday, it was now too hot for me to continue working. I would sit in the shade under one of the giant plane trees with a bottle of water I had left overnight in the bar's freezer in order to recover a bit before returning to the venta for a cool shower and the *menú del día* and a few valued snatches of conversation with Carmen.

I noticed that my body was slowly beginning to change. I was no longer the pasty-faced, feeble-looking foreigner who had arrived from god only knew where a few weeks before. Now I was beginning to tan and beginning to grow muscles where I had never had any before. The work had been impossibly hard for me at first, but I was now starting to get used to it and my body no longer ached through the afternoons as it had done at first.

Every morning when I started work, I wondered if it might finally be the day that I would uncover some clue as to the whereabouts of the gold. Every time I came across a slight depression in the ground my heart jumped at the possibility that this might be the place. I'd even begun digging a couple of times in the early days. But, the more I cleared away, the more I realised that the plot of land was covered in hundreds of lumps and bumps, and so I decided not to do any more digging until I had the whole area cleared.

After the first couple of week's work, I began to uncover the ruins of the old farmhouse. All that remained were some low stone walls just a few feet high and the brown-tiled floors of the rooms. It hadn't been a big house, but then in times gone by whole families of ten or twelve would all have crowded into the very smallest of spaces, and people back then liked to have plenty of children to help on the land.

I liked to imagine this place as a bustling family home, with the father and his army of strapping sons working the land, growing their vegetables in neat rows, tending their vines and fruit trees, selling any surplus they could produce at the local market in San Antonio, the mother and daughters looking after the hens and maybe a few pigs, washing and mending clothes, the permanent smell of something always cooking in a big pot on the fire, and the family donkey idly walking round and round in circles to work the pump to draw water from the ground. A few days later, not far from the ruined house I found the well, and then just beyond that I began to find masses of tangled old vines, stretching from the house down the slope towards the stream. Left unattended for so long the vines had grown long like thick snakes along the ground, and I was amazed to see that there were signs of new shoots beginning to grow through.

I hurried to find one of my elderly neighbours in the next plot and brought him back with me to look at what I had uncovered. He scratched the stubble on his cheek for a while as he contemplated the ruins of my vineyard.

"My grandfather always used to say that this place had the best vines for miles around, being so close to the stream and with this slope in the sun and everything."

"Really?"

"Yes. Everyone said that it was a terrible waste this land just being left unattended, but none of us had the money to buy it back in the seventies. Times were hard."

"So, the question is, is there anything I can do to save the vines?" I asked him. He shrugged.

"Maybe, who knows? There's an awful lot of work to be done here and they haven't been pruned for generations, who knows how they'll react – it's amazing that they're still growing."

"They can't have been planted before the Civil War can they?"

"Maybe, my vines were. My grandfather replanted in the early thirties, I expect all the neighbours would have done it at the same time, all helped each other out."

"So, vines can live that long?"

"Sure, they can survive for generations, but yours' are going to need a lot of extra care."

He invited me over to his plot next door to look at his vineyard, so that I could get an idea of how one ought to look. It was immaculate, neat north to south rows of clipped and manicured plants, a few selected shoots reaching along wires to keep the fruit off the ground. There were buds already forming everywhere I looked.

I decided to make the vineyard my number one priority for the next few days, to see if I could get it into some sort of order and who knows, maybe I might get some sort of crop in the autumn. Who was I trying to kid? I knew nothing about farming whatsoever. But then, somewhere inside me I was rather attracted to the idea of growing my own grapes

181

that could be turned into my own wine. Imagine opening a bottle of your own wine! The more I thought about it the better it seemed and the more determined I became. I decided to come back to the finca in the afternoons as well, in an effort to get the vineyard tidied as soon as possible. I left immediately and headed for Los Rosales to get some wooden stakes and some wire in order to trail them as soon as I had cut them back. I was a man with an exciting new project and it felt good. I even forgot about the gold, well, almost.

*

It had been a long afternoon's work, toiling, back bent under a hot sun. My bare torso was covered with sweat, and there was sweat running down my forehead, mixing with my factor 50 sun cream and stinging my eyes. I'd nearly finished clipping a row of vines and I wanted to get them strung before I left. The shadows of the plane trees were lengthening across the land, but it was still very hot. I thought back just briefly to my last winter in London and my trips to Edinburgh and the extreme cold there, and it was strange to think about that here in this parched field so far away.

I stood and straightened my back and took off my ridiculous hat to wipe away the sweat from my forehead for the thousandth time. Then, over by the road, I spotted the figure of a person, watching me. Whoever it was raised a hand and waved in greeting. I squinted hard through the heat haze and realised that it was Carmen. It was her day off, the Venta was closed all day on Mondays, which forced me to do my own thing as far as food was concerned. This normally meant a doughnut for breakfast, a trip to the bar in the village square for lunch and a cured ham sandwich from the village shop for tea. I was allowed to help myself to bottles of beer from the fridge in the Venta's bar so that I didn't die of thirst, and I just left a euro for everyone I took beside the till.

I wondered what Carmen was doing out here. I guessed that she was just cycling past on her way somewhere and had decided to check out my finca. We chatted every day, whenever things were slow at the venta, and I gave her progress reports on how my land clearance was going, so she must have got curious to see exactly what the foolish, tongue-tied foreigner had been up to every day. I put down my clippers and walked slowly across the uneven ground, past the ruins of the farmhouse, towards the road where she was standing.

"Hi there," she called out as I approached.

"What brings you all the way out here?" I asked.

"You do, *tonto*, I went to find you at the venta but Antonio said you were working here in the afternoons now too." Antonio also lived at the venta, he had done ever since his wife had run away with a travelling salesman who occasionally stopped by for lunch, but I rarely saw him on his day off, since we both liked to keep to ourselves.

"What did you want to see me about?" I asked nervously.

"I just wanted to see you, *tonto,* is that okay?" she laughed. She must have seen the blank, disbelieving look that took over my face. "We don't get much of a chance to talk while I'm working, so I thought I'd come and see you and we could spend the evening together. When I heard you were here I decided to cycle over. I've brought a picnic and some wine, I hope that's okay?"

"That's great," I responded, not quite able to believe what was happening.

"So, are you going to show me around or not?" she wanted to know, flashing me that smile of hers'.

"There isn't much to see," I told her, "But sure, come on." She left her bicycle at the side of the road and we set off together towards the ruins of the old house. Beyond that I showed her where the well had been, and then we were into the vineyard that I was about half way through clearing.

"Do you need a bit of help to finish up?" she offered.

"Okay, I want to get this last row strung up before I call it a night." I hammered the wooden stakes into the hard ground and tossed her some gloves so that she could trail the wire along behind me. It didn't take long, and soon we were sitting in my usual spot under the plane trees on some old cardboard boxes I had flattened out. The wine she had brought from the venta was still a little chilled and I drank it gratefully from a plastic glass. She confessed that Antonio had given her the food when she had told him that she intended to cycle out to see me. There was some cut ham and cheese, a small plastic container of potato salad with mayonnaise and some *carne mechada*. I felt a tiny bit guilty that we might be eating Antonio's supper, but Carmen just laughed and said that the man was a chef and the venta's kitchen was stocked full of stuff. Besides, Antonio had put on a lot of weight since his wife had left him and if he didn't eat anything at all for a week it wouldn't do him any harm.

The mention of Antonio's erstwhile wife reminded me that I didn't know anything about Carmen's personal life. I knew that every man, single or not, who came to eat at the venta flirted outrageously with her, but I also knew that she kept them at a distance. No one had ever mentioned to me that she might be seeing someone, so I asked her if there was anyone special in her life. Suddenly her face became uncharacteristically serious and I wished for the life of me that I hadn't asked.

"I was married," she said quietly after a strong silence throughout which she had looked intently into my eyes. "It didn't last long. He used to beat me," she whispered looking away now. I didn't say anything. I didn't know what to say. How could anyone want to beat this beautiful, charming woman? Eventually she decided to continue, again in a whisper. "I used to work in a bar and he thought I was flirting with all the customers and he used to get mad and when I got home he would fly into a rage and start to hit me. He was always crazy jealous, and when he had been out drinking I sometimes thought he would kill me."

"So you left him?"

"Yes, it wasn't easy. I went to my mother's house for a while but he soon found me there. He was drunk and he tried to break the door down. He said he was going to kill me. So I called the police and when they took him away I fled. I ended up here."

"I'm sorry," I said.

"What about you?" she asked with a sigh, looking directly at me again. "Have you got someone special waiting for you back in England?"

"No. I used to be married, but she left me for someone else. We got divorced."

"Is that why you decided to come to Spain?"

"No, not really I inherited this land from my father, and I wanted to come out here to see what it was like. I was stuck in a dead-end job and I was fed up of feeling sorry for myself I guess."

"How long will you stay?" she asked.

"I don't know. I've certainly nothing to go back to," I told her and it suddenly dawned on me that this was the painful truth.

Carmen refilled our plastic glasses with wine and then lit a cigarette. She smoked foul-smelling black tobacco because they were the cheapest cigarettes you could buy. I had always hated smoking, but somehow she managed to make it seem sexy, holding the cigarette in her long thin fingers and exhaling the smoke through her long thin nose. I put my wine down on the ground and got up to make a little heap of vine clippings, and then, using her lighter, I set a piece of cardboard alight and got a little fire going. It wasn't cold or anything, at least not for me, but it was very romantic sitting there in the darkness, watching the flames dancing before us. She moved towards me after a while, leaning her slender upper body against mine and neither of us spoke. I wondered if she wanted me to kiss her as much as I wanted to. It was without doubt the happiest I could ever remember being in my whole life.

TWENTY-NINE

Towards the end of June I had the plot of land completely cleared and a new stone wall had been built along the front by the road with a metal gate in the middle. A couple of unemployed builders who usually whiled away their afternoons in the bar of the venta had done it for me on the cheap – at least that's what they said. Early every day a lorry had arrived from the local quarry and the two men had worked all morning until their supply of stones ran out. It took a couple of weeks to complete, but it looked good now that it was finally done. It gave the place a cared-for look that it hadn't had for a long, long time. My vines were growing nicely too, the tiny clusters of grapes already beginning to form. I had a mini inspection tour of the vineyard first thing every morning, and was always amazed by what I saw. I didn't like to get carried away or anything but I was so looking forward to that first sip of my own vintage.

At the beginning of the last week of June, I got some bad news from Antonio, the owner of the Quinto Pino, that my rent would have to go up considerably in the peak season. He was very apologetic and offered me the biggest discount he could on normal summer prices, but he said that renting out rooms for the high season was how he made most of his money for the year. I decided I would have to talk to Carmen about it.

Most evenings I would sit at the bar with a beer waiting for her to finish work and then I would drive her back to her little house in the village. More often than not I would spend the night and lie awake beside her, listening to her soft breathing as the light breeze that came through the open window played intermittently across my face. I never tired of telling myself how lucky I was. Anyway, I told Carmen about what Antonio had said about my rent.

"Do you think you could talk to him about it?" I asked her, since everyone knew she had a lot of influence over him.

"Why don't you just move in here for the summer?" she offered.

"Really, what here, with you?"

"Of course with me, *tonto*, who do you want to move in with? You practically live here anyway, don't you?"

"I guess so."

"That's settled then. Move in whenever you like. I'll give you a key in the morning. Now shut up and go to sleep."

And so the next day, I packed my meagre possessions into my meagre car and moved in with Carmen. And every afternoon, I still had lunch at the venta and afterwards we would while away the hottest hours of the day lying naked on the bed with the fan on hurricane setting.

When Carmen had to return to the venta in the late afternoons I would go back out to the finca and continue with my work. I had decided that the best way to find the gold was to go about it in a methodical manner, just as Howard Carter had done in the Valley of the Kings. With string and wooden stakes I divided the front part of the land up into squares of five metres by five metres, and I was going to scan them with a metal detector one after the other, crossing each square off on my master plan as it was done. If the Republican gold was buried somewhere here then I was determined to find it.

In the first square of land I wasted a lot of time digging up a myriad of useless small pieces of metal. I wasn't used to using the metal detector and I had the settings all wrong. It would have been perfect for finding dropped coins on the beach or something, but here in the middle of the countryside it was turning up bent old forks, metal buttons, buried tin cans and small bits of broken farm implements. After the first square took almost forever, I adjusted the settings to the minimum level of detection after all if it went over a metal crate full of gold it was not going to miss it. In fact, it would probably blow my bloody ears off.

When I finished a row of squares I would set up the next lot and so I slowly moved back further away from the road. It was boring, time-consuming work, and of course every now and then I would get a false alarm and have to dig a hole in the ground, only to be rewarded with a rusty piece of coil or a bucket full of holes. I found the head of an old spade, a broken saw blade and a bent spoon to go with my collection of forks.

I hadn't told anyone what I was doing, not even Carmen. I didn't want the secret of the gold to get out, who knows how many people might suddenly turn out in the middle of the night armed with metal detectors and shovels and start digging holes all over the place.

However, my activities didn't go unnoticed for too long. Manolo, the bread delivery guy, suddenly screeched to a halt one morning in a cloud of dust and got out of his van to come to inspect my land which he hadn't seen for a while. As he opened the gate he saw me, head down, earphones on, scanning a square not far from the two giant plane trees, which would have been a good reference point for someone who wanted to bury some gold I had suddenly realised. Manolo must have called out to me, but when I didn't respond he simply bounded over and slapped both his huge hands onto my upper back almost toppling me over and scaring the shit out of me. I jumped out of my skin and screamed at the top of my voice, so loud that it could have been heard for miles around.

"What the fuck are you doing?" he wanted to know.

"Shit Manolo, you almost scared me half to death," I panted, holding my hand over my heart to stop it exploding. I had known that this moment was bound to arrive someone was bound to find out that I was using a metal detector to look for something, and so I had a ready-prepared excuse.

"I'm looking for Roman coins," I told him.

"Really?" he asked doubtfully.

"Sure, this area used to be swarming with Romans. Some coins are worth a fortune you know."

"If you say so."

"Yes, yes I do, I'm a bit of an expert you see," I lied, "Roman artefacts have always been a bit of a hobby of mine." Manolo just nodded his head sadly.

"So, how many coins have you found oh great finder of Roman artefacts?"

I set the metal detector gently down on the ground and slowly reached into the pocket of my shorts. Carefully, so as not to drop my hoard, I pulled out my handful of coins.

"You mustn't tell anybody about this Manolo," I warned him, "not even Carmen, *vale*?"

"Okay *inglés*, whatever you say. Now show me what you've found."

Slowly I opened my hand to reveal the five coins I had found so far. Manolo leaned in to get a close look at my little treasure collection. It took him a minute or so to realise that none of them were Roman. The coins were all pre-civil war Spanish coins, all small denominations and worth next to nothing, certainly not worth all the time and effort I had put into finding them.

"Those aren't Roman," stated Manolo and he looked at me as if I were crazy.

"I know that," I said, "but it's just a matter of time until I start to find some Roman stuff."

Manolo nodded doubtfully. He didn't stay much longer. I offered him a cold beer from my cooler but he said he had a lot of deliveries still left to make, starting with the venta, and off he went, back across the uneven ground towards his van.

"Remember," I called after him, "don't tell anyone about this."

"Yeah, sure," he called back over his shoulder. I went to sit under the nearest plane tree with a cool beer whilst I left the metal detector's battery pack charging for a bit plugged into the generator. I wondered just how long Manolo would be able to keep my activities a secret. When I finished my beer, I started the little pump that was also plugged into the generator, to fill the metal trough I had for washing with water from the stream. There was a long plastic pipeline that snaked down through the vineyard, and in the evenings, after my final wash of the day, I would fill a bucket to use the water on the vines, just a little plastic cup-full at the base of each plant.

When I arrived at the venta for lunch, I instantly realised just how long Manolo had been able to keep the Roman coins ruse a secret.

"Ah, Julius Caesar," called out Antonio from the kitchen when he saw me, "hard day at the senate?"

I decided to go out onto the terrace, as far away from the kitchen as I could. Carmen appeared soon enough with a bottle of *tinto* and another of *casera* and put them down on my table.

"Coins then?" she stated matter-of-factly.

"Yeah," I lied.

"Okay, you have lunch and then when we get home you tell me the truth," and she disappeared back towards the kitchen. She hadn't bothered to tell me what was on the menu, she would just bring me whatever she thought I should eat she'd been doing that for some time.

After I had eaten, I sat at the bar with a coffee and waited for Carmen to finish with the last few customers who were taking an eternity over their ice cream as if they had nothing else planned for the rest of the day. I was desperately trying to wrack my brains to come up with some plausible lie to fob Carmen off with, but the more I thought about it, the more I realised that she wouldn't be put off by anything but the truth. At the end of the day, if there was to be any future for my relationship with Carmen it would have to be built on trust, and that meant the truth. I would have to tell her the whole incredible story about the Spanish Republic's lost gold and trust her to keep it a secret from everyone else, especially from the likes of Manolo.

When we eventually got home we stripped our clothes off and got into the shower together as we always did, and then we lay on the bed in front of the fan to dry off. After about ten minutes of silence Carmen turned towards me, propping up her face with her hand to look at mine.

"So, the real reason you've got a metal detector and are wasting your time out in the middle of the countryside is?"

"You won't believe me if I tell you," I said.

"Sure I will. Just tell me."

And so I told her the story of the last lorry to leave besieged Madrid back in March 1939 heading for a rendezvous with a Mexican ship in Alicante. I told her about the Republican General who had been waiting for them and about his gold. She gasped when I mentioned the word gold. I then told her that my grandfather had been the captain in charge of the mission and that the English nurse, Elizabeth, had been my grandmother and she had been the one who had purchased the finca where I was now working, shortly after the death of Franco.

"So you think that the gold is buried somewhere on your land then?"

"Yes, that's exactly what I think. That's why I'm here to find the last Republican gold."

"What a lot of crap," laughed Carmen. "No wonder everyone thinks you're fucking crazy."

I got up from the bed and went over to my drawer in her chest of drawers and pulled out my grandfather's diary from its hiding place behind my pants and socks.

"Here," I said, "this is the proof, read it and then decide if you think I'm crazy or not."

"I don't read English, *tonto*," she snapped obviously beginning to lose patience with me.

"It's in Spanish," I told her, "my grandfather was bilingual. His father was English but his mother was Spanish." She snatched the diary from me and began to read. I rolled over onto my back and I must have fallen asleep because the next thing I knew was Carmen shaking me to wake me up several hours later.

"It's time to get up lazy bones."

"So, what do you think of the diary?" I wanted to know.

"It's interesting but I haven't finished it yet. I'll carry on with it later."

And so I dropped Carmen back at the venta and drove on towards the Finca El Dorado. On the way I questioned whether I was in fact crazy to be obsessed with the thought of finding gold here. What would I do if it turned out to be a total waste of time? Should I just go back to England with my tail between my legs and never tell anyone what I had been doing here in Spain?

As I neared the bend I saw a 4x4 parked on the side of the road and two men standing by my new entrance gate obviously looking at my plot of land. I wondered what they could possibly want. Had word got around that there was a secret hoard of priceless Roman coins waiting to be found? Surely Carmen hadn't had time to tell anyone about the real reason for my being there?

THIRTY

I parked my old SEAT behind the 4x4 and got slowly out to face the two men. Maybe they were undercover policemen come to ask me about valuable coins I had found and not handed over to the proper authorities. Perhaps they were dealers in Roman antiquities about to make me a breathtaking offer for any future treasure I might unearth.

When I saw the two men up close I realised that they were both dressed in dirty workday clothes and that one was considerably older than the other. The older man stretched out his hand in greeting.

"I'm José, *el vecino*," he said gesturing to the far side of my finca which obviously bordered his land. We had never previously spoken, although I had seen him sometimes in the mornings, far away, tending his vegetables. He wasn't the neighbour who had taken me to see his vines he was the one with the plot on the other side.

"*Encantado*," I answered, shaking his strong, callused hand.

"*Mi hijo*," he informed me, gesturing towards the younger man. I shook the son's hand too.

"What can I do for you?" I asked nervously.

"We were wondering if you might possibly be looking to sell this land," said my neighbour.

"Not that it's worth much," said the son helpfully.

"*Mi hijo* is looking for somewhere to farm and we thought that this plot would be ideal. That way, when I finally go to the great *finca* in the sky, he can join the two plots together you see."

"I see. And what kind of money are we talking about?" I asked as casually as I could.

"We are poor people, *muy pobres,*" said the old man with an apologetic shrug of his hunched shoulders.

"And this is poor land really, for farming," added the son.

"So, we were thinking of say, maybe, *cincuenta millones*," offered the old man.

"Fifty million!" I spluttered like an idiot, not quite able to believe my ears. Were they serious? For fifty million they could have the land right away, gold and all. Then it suddenly dawned on me that we weren't talking Euros here and I felt like a complete idiot. I had heard conversations in the venta about house and land purchases, and the prices were always agreed in pesetas first and then calculated into Euros. I tried to do a quick calculation in my head. What the fuck was 50 million divided by 167? I realised that the answer wasn't going to come out of my brain any time soon, so I pulled out my mobile phone and selected the calculator option and it worked it out as more or less 300,000 Euros.

"So, what do you think?" asked my neighbour.

"It's a fair price," added the son.

"I'm sure it is," I said. "Listen, this is all a bit of a surprise. I hadn't given any thought to selling the land I've only just got here really. I'll need some time to think about it, if that's okay? How does a week sound?"

"A week? Okay, we'll come back in a week," said the son. They both shook my hand and then left in their muddy 4x4.

I went to sit under a plane tree to drink a coke and to try to take onboard this quite unexpected turn of events. If there was no gold buried here then this offer of purchase could well be my best way out of my current situation. I could sell up, return to England and have enough money to buy a little house and maybe to start my own business or something, although I had no ideas as to what kind of business as yet. It was quite an attractive thought and I let it play around my brain for the rest of the evening as I scanned another couple of squares with the metal detector without too much enthusiasm. The further away from the road I got the more I became convinced that there wasn't any gold here at all. Why hadn't my grandfather just drawn a bloody map?

At last I finished up for the night, watered the vines as I always did and drove back to the venta to pick up Carmen. When we got back to the house she went to get the diary and sat down to read while I prepared a tuna salad. I poured us both a glass of local red wine and felt a little twinge of guilt as I took a sip and realised that I might be about to betray my own vines. A serious debate was going on in my head as to whether or not I should tell Carmen about my neighbour's offer to purchase the land, but since I hadn't made up my own mind yet I decided to keep it to myself for a bit.

After we had eaten, Carmen went back to reading the diary whilst I pretended to watch a film on TV. When the film came to an end I asked Carmen if she was ready for bed.

"You go on up," she replied, "I'm going to finish reading this. Oh, by the way, if there is gold out there and you do find it, what are you going to do with it?"

"I'm going to return it to the legitimate Spanish Government, that's what my grandfather wanted, that's what he risked his life for."

"So, you're doing all this for nothing."

"No, I'm doing it for my grandfather and for all those who helped him."

"Maybe they'll give you some kind of finder's fee or a medal or something."

"I don't know," I answered with a shrug.

And so I went upstairs, and within a few minutes I was asleep. The fresh air, the farm work and the red wine had all taken their toll on me, as they did every day. Carmen woke me up at some stage in the middle of the night.

"Okay, I believe you," she whispered.

"What?" I asked still half asleep.

"The gold, I believe you that your grandfather might have buried the gold at the finca."

"You do?"

"Yes, I thought you were mad at first, but when I read the diary it all started to make sense. Why else would your grandmother want to purchase that bit of worthless land out in the middle of nowhere?"

"The only thing is that I can't find the gold," I told her.

"But you haven't given up looking have you?"

"No, I'm still looking, of course I am it's just that I thought I would have found it by now. The further I get away from the road the less hope I have left. Still, Howard Carter found the tomb of Tutankhamen in the last place he had left to look, so who knows?"

"It must be there somewhere."

"I hope so I'm going to feel like a bit of an idiot if it isn't."

"You're not an idiot," she said and she reached for me and embraced me to her, crushing my head into her chest. Suddenly, I wasn't sleepy anymore. My grandfather's diary that she had been holding slipped from her hand and tumbled forgotten to the floor as I rolled on top of her and pressed my mouth to hers'.

*

The next morning I awoke to the sound of the shower. I sat up in bed and waited for Carmen to finish. When she came out I got out of bed. She saw the diary lying on the floor next to her side of the bed. She bent to pick it up.

"There was one thing I wanted to ask you," she said. "There was something written at the back which I didn't understand. Now, where was it," and she began to flick through the empty unwritten pages at the end of the diary. "I guess it's in English."

She eventually found what she was looking for and handed the diary to me. It was open at about the seventh or eighth blank page and right at the bottom my grandfather had written 'all's well that ends well.' Without warning my legs just gave way beneath me and I slumped backwards onto the bed as if I'd been hit by a speeding truck. I was breathless with shock.

"Are you all right?" asked Carmen a worried look on her face.

"I know where the gold is," I finally managed to gasp.

"You do? What does it say?"

I translated the phrase for her into Spanish and of course it meant nothing to her at all, just as my grandfather would have known. This message was as good as a map, but would only be of use to someone who knew the Finca El Dorado. I quickly explained to her that the word 'well' had another meaning, apart from the obvious one of something being good, a place to draw water from deep in the ground.

"*Un pozo?*" she questioned.

"Yes, *un pozo.*"

"But there's a well at the finca."

"Yes."

"Oh my god!" exclaimed Carmen and she suddenly slumped down beside me on the bed her hand clasped across her mouth.

*

I dropped Carmen off at the venta just a little bit later than usual, but not late enough to cause any suspicion. Our joint first instinct had obviously been to jump in my car and head for the finca and look down the well, but after some discussion we decided that it was best to go prepared and also not let anyone think that something out of the ordinary was afoot. It was with enormous will power that I turned my car around in front of the venta and headed for Los Rosales. We had decided that we were going to need a ladder, a powerful light and some sort of winch or pulley system if we were going to get the heavy crates out of the dried up well. Neither of us doubted for a second now that we would find them there waiting for us. What difference could a few more hours make?

I spent the morning in Los Rosales. I hadn't been there for a while, so I checked up on my bank account and then had a long leisurely coffee around mid morning sitting at a table outside a little bar in the main square, trying to enjoy the sunshine, but all the time with my pulse racing and my nerves on edge. Had I still been in the village I would not have been able to resist the temptation to head out for the finca and stick my head down the well to try to see what was inside. Suddenly, for the first time since deciding that the well was my grandfather's chosen hiding place, I began to have doubts. What if he had just used the phrase to sort of sum up the fact that he had somehow managed to escape from defeated Republican Spain against all the odds? I was going to look a right idiot in front of Carmen if I climbed down into the well and discovered it to be empty. And I realised that I really did care about looking an idiot in front of Carmen, it was something I really didn't want to do.

I left it as late as I could to leave Los Rosales and head for lunch at the venta. I knew it was going to seem like forever waiting for Carmen to finish up after lunch. I had bought everything we thought we needed at my usual ironmongers and had the ladder poking between the front seats as I drove back.

*

As soon as she could Carmen finished up at work and we headed for the finca. I pulled up by the gate and handed her the key for the padlock. Normally I just left my car in the road, but this afternoon I hoped I would be able to fill the boot with gold coins. Once we had reached the well we unloaded the things I had bought and set about inspecting the old wooden cover that lay across the well. It was splintered and broken and after trying to prise it open a couple of times I set to it with my sledgehammer

196

and smashed a hole big enough for a man to get through. I took the huge torch I had bought and began to shine it down the shaft. The shaft was lined with bricks and disappeared eventually into dried mud at the bottom. I couldn't see any crates of gold. A wave of panic shot through me, and then I tried to reassure myself that my grandfather would never have left them visible but would have tried to bury them.

"What can you see?" Carmen wanted to know.

"Nothing yet," I replied. "Let's get the ladder and I can go down and get a look at the bottom."

We extended the ladder as long as it would go and then dropped it into the well shaft. Once I was reasonably sure that it was on a secure footing I took my spade and began to climb down. Carmen held the torch at the top of the shaft so that I could see what I was doing. Once I got to the bottom I began to scrape away at the loose surface of earth and suddenly the head of the spade hit metal. I banged it again just to make sure.

"I think I've found something," I called up the shaft towards Carmen.

"What is it?"

"It's something metallic. I'm going to have to dig it out." I began to push earth away furiously from the object I had discovered and soon the corner of a rusty metal crate came into view. As soon as I saw it my heart leapt into my mouth. It was exactly what I had been hoping to find.

"It's a crate," I shouted up.

"Oh my god!" came Carmen's scream of response.

With my hands I began to pull away the earth from around the sides of the crate until I had it all in view. There was a rusted padlock holding it closed. I climbed quickly back up the ladder to the surface and Carmen helped me to set up the tripod for the pulley system I had purchased. I looped some rope over the pulley and then took the end to the bottom of the well and tied it to the crate through the ancient padlock. Once back at the surface Carmen and I pulled on the rope with all our strength. Slowly the crate began to free itself from its earthy grave and we hauled it up the shaft. When it came into view Carmen gave a gasp and almost let go of the rope in her excitement.

I managed to swing the crate over towards the side of the shaft and then we set it down on the ground. We both stood and looked down at it for a while wondering if there really could be gold inside.

197

"How do we open it?" asked Carmen. I thought for a second and then picked up my sledgehammer.

"Stand back," I told her as I raised the heavy implement up to my shoulder. I took a quick breath and then brought the sledgehammer smashing down against the padlock. There was a frightening crash of metal against metal and then the lock broke and fell away. I dropped to my knees beside the crate. Carmen knelt down beside me her hand covering her mouth a look of fear in her eyes.

I reached out and touched the lid with shaking hands. Here I was about to open something that had been locked closed eighty years before, something that people had given their lives to protect or to try to steal. I suddenly realised that my mouth was dry and I couldn't swallow.

I pushed up the lid and it fell backwards on its hinges against the other side. For a few seconds time stood still as we got our first look at the contents of that first crate.

"Oh shit," was the only thing I could think of to say.

"What is it?" asked Carmen.

I reached forward, my fingers shaking more violently than before, and touched the jagged contents of what had been stored in the crate. It was rubble from some old building. A few broken brown bricks, some small chunks of grey marble and jagged pieces of smashed concrete. No doubt they came from one of the bombed out buildings of civil war Madrid.

"It's only the first one," whispered Carmen, although she knew as well as I did that we were never going to find any gold now. Someone had taken the gold and filled the crates with rubble long before my grandfather ever became involved with it.

We both stood up and turned to face each other. Carmen threw her arms around me and held me to her. It was strange, but my overriding feeling was one of tremendous relief. If the truth be known, I had been terrified of actually finding any gold. I had enjoyed looking for it. I had enjoyed my trip down through Spain and I was happier living in San Antonio than I had ever been in my entire life, but the search for gold had simply become an excuse for not returning to England. But the search had lasted just long enough for me to realise that I didn't want to return, I wanted to stay here in this godforsaken place but most of all with the wonderful woman I had fallen in love with.

198

"I'm so sorry," whispered Carmen. "I know how badly you wanted to find that gold for your grandfather's sake."

I held her at arms' length and looked into her eyes.

"It doesn't matter. I came here to search for gold, but I ended up finding something a lot more valuable – happiness. I think my grandfather would have approved."

*

It's a couple of years later now and Carmen and I have just finished building a little house on our land. The well is in working condition again now that I've removed all the rusty crates that were in there. I had all the rubble buried in the concrete foundations of our farmhouse which stands in the same place in the middle of the finca where there always used to be a house. I grow vegetables which I sell to the local shops and ventas and we keep a few chickens.

In the evenings, after a hard day's work in the fields under the cruel sun, I like nothing better than to sit out on the porch watching the sun go down with a glass of my own wine. In those last few moments of daylight the colour of the earth changes and takes on a strange golden hue, and it is easy to see why this place was called Finca El Dorado long before it was ever the possible resting place for the last gold of the Spanish Republic. Sometimes my little son comes to sit upon my knee and we stay there together wrapped up in the beauty of nature, the only sounds coming from the kitchen as Carmen moves around as she prepares something for us to eat when we finally go inside.

About the Author

Kelvin Hughes lives in the South of Spain with his wife and two children. He studied Spanish and French at university and has been a language teacher for over twenty years. The Last Lorry is his first novel.

Follow on Facebook: Kelvin Hughes - Writer

Printed in Great
Britain
by Amazon